A FIELD GUIDE TO
AUSTRALIAN
ORCHIDS
EPIPHYTES
INCLUDING THE ISLAND TERRITORIES

Sarcochilus hillii.

A FIELD GUIDE TO AUSTRALIAN ORCHIDS

EPIPHYTES

INCLUDING THE ISLAND TERRITORIES

David L. Jones

B.Ag.Sci., Dip. Hort.

Durabaculum phalaenopsis.

CONTENTS

Preface 6

Acknowledgements 7

How to Use this Book 8

Glossary 12

Introduction 16

Epiphytes and Lithophytes

GROUP 1 The *Bulbophyllum* alliance (*Adelopetalum, Blepharochilum, Cirrhopetalum, Ephippium, Fruticicola, Kaurorchis, Oncophyllum, Oxysepala, Papulipetalum, Serpenticaulis, Sestochilos*) 30

GROUP 2 The *Dendrobium* alliance – 1 (Tribe Dendrobieae – *Ceraia, Coelandria, Dendrobium*)

GROUP 3 The *Dendrobium* alliance – 2 (Tribe Grastidiinae – *Australorchis, Cadetia, Davejonesia, Dichopus, Diplocaulobium, Dockrillia, Durabaculum, Eleutheroglossum, Flickingeria, Grastidium, Sayeria, Stilbophyllum, Thelychiton, Trachyrrhizum, Tropilis*) 56

GROUP 4 The *Vanda* alliance (*Bogoria, Chiloschista, Drymoanthus, Luisia, Micropera, Microtatorchis, Mobilabium, Peristeranthus, Phalaenopsis, Plectorrhiza, Pomatocalpa, Rhinerrhiza, Robiquetia, Saccolabiopsis, Sarcanthopsis, Sarcochilus, Schoenorchis, Taeniophyllum, Thrixspermum, Trachoma, Trichoglottis, Vanda*) 128

GROUP 5 Miscellaneous epiphytes (*Acriopsis, Appendicula, Blepharoglossum, Bryobium, Cestichis, Coelogyne, Cymbidium, Dipodium, Oberonia, Octarrhena, Phreatia, Pinalia, Thelasis*) 178

GROUP 6 Island Territories 203

Further reading 219

Index to scientific names 220

Index to common names 222

PREFACE

We are fortunate in Australia to have such an amazing diversity of plants which have adapted to the bioregions of all parts of the continent. Prominent among the Australian flora are our cherished and unique orchids, which are so diverse and different that people, including international visitors, travel long distances each year to see these treasures growing in their natural habitat. Native orchids hold a special fascination for me, and I have been very fortunate to be able to study and write about them for much of my life.

The generally positive reaction to my latest book on native orchids (*A Complete Guide to Native Orchids of Australia*, Third Edition, 2021) was gratifying and, although unwieldy and expensive, I was pleasantly surprised to learn that it sold out within 12 months of publication. Frequent comments made about its large size, weight and impracticality for use in the field, prompted the spawning of two smaller field guides that deal separately with the terrestrials and epiphytes. The most challenging part of preparing these guides has been meeting the wordage limitations imposed by the enforced reduction in size, while still producing a useful but necessarily abbreviated text to support the photographs and enable identification of orchids in the wild. Although relatively small, these new books are comprehensive and cover all the species and include many of the photographs from the larger book. Taxonomic changes that have resulted from recent studies are included and several photographs have been replaced by better quality and/or more informative images.

All epiphytic genera are included in this book and, as in the earlier big book, related and familiar orchids, such as the sarcanths, are grouped together to make identification easier. Within each grouping, the genera and species are mostly arranged alphabetically, however, in some large or complex genera, such as *Sarcochilus*, related or similar species are grouped together to assist with identification. A glossary is included to explain the few botanical terms used in the book. A bibliography of some important botanical papers and local field guides is presented for those who wish to learn more about these amazing products of evolution while they still exist.

Opposite: *Thelychiton speciosus* subsp. *speciosus*.

ACKNOWLEDGEMENTS

I thank the many people who supported my research over the years and contributed in various ways to this book.

Special thanks to my wife Barbara for her calming influence, patience, help with numerous finicky chores and cheerful companionship at home and in the field. Also appreciated is the support and technical help of my daughter Sandie and son Tim. Thanks to Jean Egan for hospitality and support of my orchid research. Also to Glenda Wood and Kelly Edwards for their friendship and marvellous help in the field.

The photographs are an important component of this book and I thank the numerous people who made theirs freely available. Special thanks to Gary Backhouse, Lachlan Copeland, Garry Brockman, Christopher French, David Banks, Mark Clements, Bruce Gray, Bill Lavarack, Mark Scott and James Walker. Others who have provided photographs include Peter McCauley and Colin Rowan.

Appreciation to Fiona Schultz and Simon Papps from New Holland Publishers for their encouragement and unstinting support of my writing , and Andrew Davies for his amazing design skills.

Finally I wish to thank all those people who contributed in various ways to the success of the three editions (published in 1988, 2006 and 2021) of my book *A Complete Guide to the Native Orchids of Australia*. Without that success, this epiphytic field guide would not have eventuated.

HOW TO USE THIS BOOK

The main aim of this book is to provide a useful guide to Australian native epiphytic orchids that is small enough to be used in the field and comprehensive enough to facilitate identification of any species found while out there. It features abbreviated descriptions and photographs for the c.240 named species found in Australia as well as those on Lord Howe Island, Norfolk Island and Christmas Island.

GENUS LAYOUT

GENERIC COMMON NAME: A group common name that links the individual species together and is a useful first step in identification.

GENERIC NAME: The botanical name of the genus in italics. The following entry includes details of the number of species in the genus, their distribution and a summary of brief pertinent botanical features that characterise the genus.

NOTES: Includes habitat details, flowering characteristics, brief notes on pollination and other points of interest.

IDENTIFICATION (IDENT:): Pointers included mainly in larger or complex genera to assist with identification to species rank.

SPECIES LAYOUT

COMMON NAME: Common names are included for all species in the hope that it will make native orchids more popular. The most appropriate common names are those that have arisen from close contact with the orchid. Confusingly, a species often has more than one common name and frequently a common name recognised in one locality is unknown in another place.

BOTANICAL NAME: The scientific name of the genus and species in italics. The botanical name consists of two parts, the first being the generic name and the second is the epithet or species name. Occasionally the taxon name of subspecies (subsp.) or variety (var.) is used, resulting in a third part to the name.

FLOWERING PERIOD: This is included in italics at the start of the entry for each species, making it easy to locate. The time of flowering is an important ecological feature and in some species can be a useful feature that can assist identification. In many species the flowering period is a guide only and flowering is influenced by external factors such as altitude, temperature and local site conditions. Anecdotal evidence is emerging of a warming climate also influencing not only flowering time, but also impacting (shortening) the length of time the flowers last.

IDENTITY (ID:): A very abbreviated summary of the major distinguishing features of the species is presented to support the photographs, which are the main means of identification used in the book. Because of limited space only useful identifying features are provided such as leaf details, floral colours and dimensions (length x width) of the main organs (pseudobulbs, leaves, inflorescence, flowers and labella).

DISTRIBUTION (Dist.:): The distribution within Australia by states and overseas from north to south and east to west; includes altitudinal range. Brief details of the main habitats where the species grows, including soils, and other points of interest such as variation, are also mentioned here.

STATUS: A very brief indication of the rarity or abundance of a species and its conservation status.

SEE ALSO: An occasional entry that is included to draw attention to similar or related species worth checking out.

OTHER FEATURES

PHOTOGRAPHS: One or two colour photographs accompany each species. Hopefully these photos will show significant features that assist with identification of the orchid involved. However, for complex groups, photos are best used in conjunction with other factors such as distribution, flowering time, habitat details and guiding notes in the text. Because of size limitations for the book, it is not possible to include photos of the variations that some orchids exhibit. The photograph caption includes the provenance of the species and the name of the photographer.

MEASUREMENTS: These are in millimetres for species under 1 metre long (e.g. 20mm) and in metres for species over 1 metre long (e.g. 1.5m). Dimensions of organs are included as length x width (mixed dimensions as 1.5m x 20mm; uniform dimensions as 600 x 20mm).

Thelychiton fleckeri Mt Lewis, Qld. D. Jones

Sarcochilus weinthalii Toowoomba, Qld. D. Banks

ABBREVIATIONS

c.	circa	**sp.**	Species (singular)
mm	millimetres	**spp.**	Species (plural)
cm	centimetres	**subsp.**	subspecies
m	metres	**var.**	variety
alt.	altitude	**Tlnd**	Tableland
hghy	highway	**Aust**	Australia
incl.	including	**ACT**	Australian Capital Territory
ined.	*ineditus* (unpublished)	**NSW**	New South Wales
infl.	inflorescence	**NT**	Northern Territory
Ck	Creek	**SA**	South Australia
CP	Conservation Park	**Vic**	Victoria
CR	Conservation Reserve	**Tas**	Tasmania
CYP	Cape York Peninsula	**NZ**	New Zealand
FP	Forest Park	**NCal**	New Caledonia
Is.	Island/s	**NG**	New Guinea
latsepetals	lateral sepals and petals	**PNG**	Papua New Guinea
ms	manuscript name	**Indon.**	Indonesia
Mt	Mount	**NE**	north-east/ern
Mtns	Mountains	**NNE**	north-north-east/ern
NFR	Native Forest Reserve	**ENE**	east-north-east/ern
NP	National Park	**NW**	north-west/ern
NR	Nature Reserve	**NNW**	north-north-west/ern
occas.	occasionally	**WNW**	west-north-west/ern
p/a lobe	Post-anther lobe	**SE**	south-east/ern
Pen.	Peninsula	**SW**	south-west/ern
R.	River	**SSW**	south-south-west/ern
Ra.	Range/s	**SSE**	south-south-east/ern
Rd	Road	**WSW**	west-south-west/ern
Rf.	Rainforest	**ESE**	east-south-east/ern
SF	State Forest	**N(n)**	north/ern
Stn	Station	**S(s)**	south/ern
Cons.	Conservation	**E(e)**	east/ern
Poll.	Pollination	**W(w)**	west/ern
Taxon.	Taxonomy	**Jan, Feb, etc**	January, February, etc

BOTANICAL NAMES OF ASSOCIATED PLANTS

The botanical names of the plants that match frequently mentioned common names found in the habitat section of the text are listed here. The names of some rarely mentioned species are generally included in the text.

Antarctic Beech	*Nothofagus moorei*
Black Paperbark	*Melaleuca lanceolata*
Black Sheoak	*Allocasuarina littoralis*
Blackwood	*Acacia melanoxylon*
Broad-leaved Paperbark	*Melaleuca viridiflora*
Brush Box	*Lophostemon confertus*
Bunya Pine	*Araucaria bidwillii*
Coachwood	*Ceratopetalum apetalum*
Cypress Pine	*Callitris* species
Eastern Leatherwood	*Eucryphia moorei*
Forest Oak	*Allocasuarina torulosa*
Freshwater Mangrove	*Barringtonia acutangula*
Gippsland Manna Gum	*Eucalyptus pryoriana*
Hoop Pine	*Araucaria cunninghamii*
Kurrajong	*Brachyton populneus*
native pine	*Callitris* species
paperbarks	*Melaleuca* species
Queensland Kauri	*Agathis robusta*
Red Beech	*Dillenia alata*
Red Cedar	*Toona ciliata*
Swamp Mahogany	*Lophostemon suaveolens*
Swamp Oak	*Casuarina glauca*
Water Gum	*Tristaniopsis laurina*

GLOSSARY OF TECHNICAL TERMS

acuminate	Tapered to a long drawn-out sharp point.
acute	Tapered a short sharp point.
aff., affinity	A botanical reference used to denote an undescribed species closely related to an already described species.
bisexual	Both male and female sexes present.
blade	The expanded part of a leaf or labellum.
bract	A leaf-like structure which lacks a blade or lamina.
bristly	With stiff hairs or bristles.
callus	A fleshy, ridged or plate-like structure found on the labellum; it may have calli, hairs or other outgrowths or be associated with nectar production.
calyx	All of the sepals of a flower.
capsule	Dry dehiscent fruit (applies to most orchids).
column	The central fleshy structure in orchid flowers composed of the style and staminal filaments.
column foot	An extension of the base of the column.
column wing	A flattened often wing-like appendage of the column which is probably a sterile stamen.
cupped	When the segments remain concave and do not become flat.
deciduous	Falling or shedding of any plant part.
decurved	Curved downwards.
deflexed	Bent sharply downwards.
denticulate	Minutely toothed.
dimorphic	Existing in two different forms.
endemic	Restricted to a particular region or country.
entire	Whole; not toothed, lobed or divided in any way.
epilithic	Growing on rocks.
epiphyte	A plant growing on or attached to another plant but not drawing nourishment from it and therefore not parasitic.

endemic	Restricted to a particular country, region or area.
evergreen	Remaining green and retaining leaves throughout the year.
falcate	Sickle-shaped.
fertile bract	A bract which subtends a pedicel.
filiform	Thread-like.
furrowed	Grooved longitudinally.
genus	A taxonomic group of closely related species.
glabrous	Without hairs.
glaucous	Covered with a bloom giving a bluish lustre.
habit	The general appearance of a plant.
habitat	The environment in which a plant grows.
indigenous	Native to a country, region or area.
inflorescence	The flowering structure of a plant.
jointed	Bearing distinct joints or nodes.
keel	A ridge like the base of a boat; such ridges may be a common adornment on the labellum callus of orchids; the midrib on the underside of the leaves of many orchids protrudes as a keel.
labellum	A lip; the third petal; in orchids and gingers the modified petal in front of the flower.
lamina	The expanded part of a leaf or labellum.
lateral lobes	The two side lobes of a labellum.
linear	Long and narrow with parallel sides.
lithophyte	A plant that grows on rocks, boulders and cliff faces.
littoral	Growing in communities near the sea.
lobe	A segment of an organ resulting from division.
marginal	Attached to or near the edge.
membranous	Thin-textured.
midlobe	The main projecting lobe of a labellum.
midrib	The principal vein that runs the full length of a leaf or segment.
monopodial	A stem with a single main axis which grows forward at the tip (as opposed to sympodial).

mycorrhiza	A beneficial relationship between the roots of a vascular plant and fungi resulting in nutrient exchange.
nectar	Sweet fluid secreted from a nectary.
nectary	Gland which secretes nectar.
node	Point on the stem where leaves or bracts arise.
non-resupinate	Orchid flower upside down (labellum above, column below).
opposite	Arising on opposite sides but at the same level.
ovary	The part of the gynoecium which encloses the ovules and after fertilisation develops into the fruit.
panicle	A branched racemose inflorescence.
papilla(e)	Small irregular pimple-like projections or bumps.
papillate, papillose	Bearing papillae.
pedicel	The stem which supports a single flower in an inflorescence.
peduncle	The main axis of a compound inflorescence or the stalk of a solitary flower which subtends the pedicel.
pelorial, peloric	An abnormality whereby the labellum is of a similar shape and colour to the other petals.
perianth	A collective term for the petals and sepals of a flower.
petal	A segment of the inner perianth whorl or corolla.
petiole	The stalk of a leaf.
plicate	Folded longitudinally in pleats.
pseudobulb	Thickened stems of sympodial orchids, sometimes bulb-like, that act as storage organs.
raceme	Simple unbranched inflorescence with stalked flowers.
recurved	Curved backwards.
reflexed	Bent sharply backward or upward.
resupinate	Orchid flower right-way-up (column above, labellum below).
rachis	The main axis of an inforescence to which the pedicels are attached.
rhizome	An underground stem with nodes, roots and which can form shoots.
scape	The peduncle and rachis of an inflorescence
seed	Mature ovule containing an embryo and capable of germinating.

sepal	Segment of the calyx or outer whorl of the perianth.
sessile	Without a stalk, pedicel or petiole.
species	A taxonomic group of closely related organisms with a common set of characters that sets them apart from another group.
spike	A simple unbranched inflorescence with sessile flowers.
spur	A slender hollow projection from a floral segment, usually on the labellum but in *Disa* it is on the dorsal sepal; spurs are often associated with nectaries.
sterile bract	A bract which does not subtend a pedicel or flower.
stigma	The enlarged sticky area that terminates the pistil is receptive to pollen and allows the pollen grains to germinate.
strand	Extended narrow growth with limited branching.
style	The slender part of the pistil which connects the stigma with the ovary; in orchids the style forms an indiscernible part of the column.
subspecies	Taxonomic rank below species and above variety.
sympodial	A growth habit whereby each stem has limited growth and new shoots arise from the base of previous shoots.
synonym	Another name for the same taxon; either an alternative name valid in a different classification system or an invalid or incorrect name.
taxon	A term used to describe any taxonomic group, for example genus and species; also a taxonomic unit that includes all species derived from a common ancestral lineage.
taxonomy	The classification of plants or animals.
tepal	Applied to sepals and petals of similar shape and size.
terete	Slender and cylindrical; circular in cross-section.
trichome	Hair-like outgrowth from surface cells.
undulate	Wavy.
variety	Taxonomic rank below subspecies and above form; taxonomic subgroup within a species used to differentiate variable populations.
vegetative	Asexual growth or propagation.
whorl	Three or more segments (leaves or flowers) in a circle at a node.
zygomorphic	Asymmetrical and irregular; a flower which cannot be divided equally in more than one plane.

INTRODUCTION TO NATIVE EPIPHYTIC ORCHIDS

Epiphytes are plants that grow above ground, using the trunks and branches of shrubs and trees to gain support and sustenance. Many species of orchids, which are the largest and most successful group of plants on the earth, are epiphytes. In fact, the majority of the Earth's orchids grow as epiphytes and a smaller contingent is found in the ground growing as terrestrials. Growing in trees as an epiphyte confers some advantages by giving the plant access to the upper levels of forests where suitable regimes of light, humidity and air movement enable their growth. Epiphytic orchids are not parasitic on the host, but they act as independent plants carrying out normal growth procedures such as respiration, photosynthesis and transpiration while obtaining water and nutrients for growth from bird droppings, detritus such as rotting plant parts and chemical compounds leached from the bark of the host. Orchids that grow on rocks are termed lithophytes but very few species of native orchids occur exclusively on rocks, most also growing as epiphytes on trees.

Australian native orchids

Most of the 1,710 or so named species of native orchids found on mainland Australia and on the island territories grow terrestrially in the ground. Some 1,470 species (86%) of native orchids are terrestrials, while the remaining 241 species (14%) grow epiphytically on trees or rocks. Of the 157 orchid genera found in Australia, 95 are terrestrial and the remaining 62 genera are epiphytes. In all some 90% of Australian orchids are endemic to the continent. Epiphytic orchids are also found on the main island territories of Lord Howe Island (four species), Norfolk Island (eight species) and Christmas Island (nine species).

Native epiphytes: Native epiphytic orchids are distributed from the tropics to temperate regions on the east coast. A small group of epiphytes is found in the northern tropical parts of the Northern Territory (6 spp.) and northern Western Australia (4 spp.), particularly near the coast. The greatest abundance and diversity of native epiphytic orchids is in the forests of Queensland (c.201 spp.), the vast majority in the north-east and reducing in numbers and diversity moving south, with a good representation in New South Wales (c.61 spp., most in the north) and very few in Victoria (5 spp.) and Tasmania (2 spp.).

Australian native epiphytes exhibit tremendous diversity in size and habit. Two species of *Oncophyllum* can be mistaken for moss and are amongst the smallest orchids in the world having growths 2–3mm across and scale-like leaves less than 1.5mm long. These miniatures, which grow in extended strands or crowded clumps, contrast with the sturdy cane-like stems of *Durabaculum brownii* which can reach more than 5m in length. Epiphytic orchids are generally evergreen and retain their leaves throughout the year, however, species which grow in seasonally harsh climates, such as *Durabaculum dicuphum*, *D. bigibbum* and *Saccolabiopsis armitii*, can shed some, or all, of their leaves in prolonged dry times to avoid periods of stress, producing new growth as the conditions improve.

Orchid flowers

Orchid flowers have three sepals and three petals in two whorls, the sepals in an outer whorl and the petals in an inner whorl. The sepals and petals can be alike or dissimilar in size, shape, colour, ornamentation and texture. When alike the sepals and petals are often referred to collectively as tepals. In orchids the front petal, known as the lip or labellum, is highly modified for the purpose of attracting vectors to ensure pollination. It can be fixed or hinged, simple or lobed, is usually quite different in size, shape and colour from the other two petals, and is often ornamented with structures such as plates, ridges, papillae, hairs and patches of colour. In some species these labellum structures produce nectar. The sexual parts of orchids are fused to form a single central fleshy structure known as the column or gynostemium. The anther (male) and stigma (female) parts remain separate on the column (anther is usually apical, stigma is central on the front) although they are often arranged in close proximity.

DS = dorsal sepal
LS = lateral sepals
P = petal
L = labellum
C = column
O = ovary

Front and side view of
Cymbidium canaliculatum
showing main floral parts

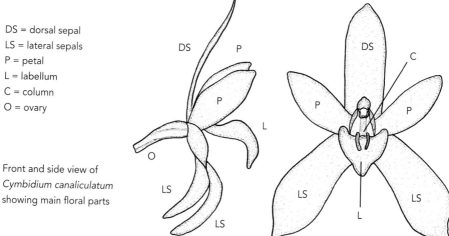

Climatic impacts and distribution

The majority of the world's orchids grow on trees as epiphytes but in Australia the reverse is true with terrestrial species dominating the orchid flora (c. 86% of native orchids grow in the ground). Epiphytic orchids are more dominant in the Australian tropics with the vast majority occurring in Queensland, however, even here their overall abundance and diversity is much less than is found in the terrestrial species.

Australian epiphytic orchids are most prolific in the wetter zones which fringe the continent where the rainfall is not only higher than inland areas but is also reliable and more evenly distributed within each region. Distribution of epiphytic orchids is mainly from coastal and near-coastal habitats to the ranges and tablelands, with a few hardy species extending to the drier scrubs on the western slopes and adjacent areas which experience less reliable rainfall and dry winters. They are much less common with increasing distance inland and are absent from far inland semi-arid to arid areas.

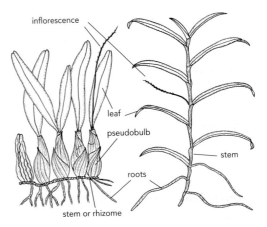

Two major growth forms of epiphytic orchids: sympodial (left), monopodial (right)

Within the higher rainfall areas of the tropics and subtropics, epiphytic orchids extend from the coastal lowlands to moderately high altitudes in the adjacent ranges, tablelands and mountain peaks (several epiphytic species are common at c.1,600m altitude on the tops of Mount Bartle Frere and Mount Bellenden Ker in northern Queensland). Epiphytic orchids are generally uncommon to rare in cool to cold temperate regions and are absent from temperate alpine and subalpine habitats. Two species of native epiphytic orchids, *Dockrillia striolata* and *Sarcochilus australis*, are known from as far south as Tasmania.

Growth habits

Two significant growth habits are readily identifiable within epiphytic orchids. In **sympodial** orchids the new growths are produced in stages, each successive growth hardening off before a new shoot is produced from its base. Orchids with this type of growth have either cane-like stems or specialised growths called pseudobulbs which are swollen stems that store water, nutrients and other compounds. In sympodial orchids the inflorescences arise from either opposite a leaf or are produced from buds near the top of each growth. In another major group of epiphytes, known as **monopodial** orchids, there are no fleshy storage organs, and the main axis of the plant increases in length steadily each year with most branching occurring from the base. In monopodial orchids the flowers are borne on inflorescences that arise from buds on the side of the main stem.

Growth cycle

Most epiphytic orchids are evergreen and have distinct periods of vegetative growth and flowering which are stimulated by specific environmental conditions such as temperature, photoperiod and rainfall. Coastal areas in the tropics and subtropics are suitably warm and wet to encourage the proliferation and growth of epiphytes. Similar expansion of epiphytic orchids also occurs in the adjacent ranges and tablelands. Some specialised epiphytic orchids have adapted to grow in less favourable climates, including monsoonal regions in which heavy rainfall is concentrated in a few summer months (the wet season) and is followed by extended winters of warm to hot weather in which no rain falls at all (the dry season). Soft new growth of the orchids

Thelychiton speciosus exhibiting sympodial growth. L. Copeland

occurs rapidly in the rainy times but then slows down and quickly hardens to cope with the changed conditions of the dry when flowering often takes place. Some epiphytic orchids may shed their leaves during extended dry times to avoid the worst impacts of dryness. A few very highly specialised epiphytic orchids are leafless, the role of photosynthesis being taken over by roots that contain chlorophyll within their tissue.

Vegetative increase

Aerial growths (keikis): Several species of native epiphytic and lithophytic orchids produce aerial growths (popularly termed keikis) from apical buds on the pseudobulbs. These reproductive growths are produced abundantly in some species such as *Durabaculum brownii*, *Thelychiton fleckeri*, *T. kingianus* and *T. moorei*, less commonly in others such *Durabaculum dicuphum* and *D. bigibbum*. The growths mature into a small swollen cane or pseudobulb with leaves and basal roots. Further development occurs with the production

Bogoria matutina exhibiting monopodial growth. D. Jones

of new growths and roots and eventually the keiki becomes a miniature plant which can grow separately when dislodged from the parent pseudobulb. Plants of *Durabaculum brownii* sometimes form tangled clumps consisting of parent canes interconnected with separately established aerial growths and developing keikis. Aerial growths of a similar nature occasionally also arise sporadically on the inflorescences of some vandaceous orchids including *Phalaenopsis rosenstromii*, *Sarcochilus ceciliae* and *S. falcatus*.

Root-tip proliferation: The leafless native epiphytes *Taeniophyllum muelleri* and *T. triquetroradix* have the ability to produce genetically identical new plants from their root tips. The new plants can in turn themselves proliferate and whole chains of clonally produced plants can be formed. This method of proliferation involves the transformation of the apical root meristem into that of a shoot meristem.

Durabaculum tattonianum and other epiphytes on paperbark, Cardwell, Qld. D. Banks

This process is more than likely influenced by plant hormones and probably occurs once the root has elongated a certain distance from the main growing point on the stem.

Special relationships

All orchids require the interaction with a suitable mycorrhizal fungus for their seeds to germinate and many species have a continuing relationship with these fungi throughout their lives, requiring reinfection at various intervals. The mycorrhizal fungus extracts nutrients from the roots of the host plant and the orchid can digest some of the fungal growths within its own root system, thus indirectly obtaining nutrients and carbon from the host plant.

Left: *Thelychiton speciosus* growing as an epiphyte on *Macrozamia communis*. A. Stephenson
Right: *Cymbidium canaliculatum* can survive in the harsh drier forests well inland from the coast. D. Banks

Pollination

Most native orchids rely on the interaction of visitors with their flowers to bring about pollination. This can be achieved in a variety of ways and is a fascinating field of study. Simple relationships involve attracting insects to the flowers by fragrance and colour and rewarding these visits with nectar. Deceit can also be involved whereby some orchid flowers, lacking nectar in this case, mimic those of other prominent plant groups which produce nectar as a reward.

Native bee visiting *Dockrillia bowmanii* flower. J. Roberts

Habitats: Epiphytic orchids favour situations where warmth, light, moisture, humidity and air movement combine to create suitable conditions for their growth. Most species are found in rainforest and wetter types of open forest from the coast to higher parts of the mountains. Rainforests are far from uniform and those occurring in cool temperate regions support a vastly different range of plants when compared with rainforests in the tropics. Habitats vary even within a rainforest and important plant growing features such as shade or sun, humidity and air movement will influence where epiphytic orchids are to be found. Many species grow on trees on the outer margins of the rainforest where light and air movement favour their growth. In dense rainforests epiphytic orchids are generally absent from lower levels in the canopy, often being found high up on the upper trunks and branches. High-altitude mountain tops and ridges exposed to buoyant air movement and receiving regular dousing with moisture from clouds, mists and fogs, often carry a wide range of interesting epiphytes and lithophytes. Even drier types of rainforest and thickets inland from the coast, that contain a range of smaller growing trees, can include specialised species. Similarly patches of forest that occur in deep gullies, rocky gorges and drier rain-shadow areas can include epiphytic orchids. Other specialised habitats, such as mangroves that fringe beaches and the saltwater parts of large rivers and coastal estuaries, littoral rainforests that develop in coastal swales, valleys and other sites close to the sea, lush dense jungles that clothe the tropical coastal lowlands and trees in large humid swamps, also support epiphytic orchids.

Epiphytes seek their own suitable niche within a particular habitat, usually favouring trees with non-shedding fibrous bark, such as paperbarks and rainforest trees. Some species require shade and humidity, growing lower down on slopes and near streams or waterfalls. Others, needing exposure to sun wind and moisture, favour the canopies of trees on mountain tops and ridges. Larger epiphytes generally prefer to grow on the trunks and

Above: *Oncophyllum globuliforme* has tiny globular pseudobulbs
1–2 mm across. D. Banks

Right: *Durabaculum brownii* has pseudobulbs that can grow 4–5 m
long. J. Roberts

larger branches of trees, some high above ground, others close to the ground. A specialised
group of small species, termed twig epiphytes, grow almost exclusively on shrubs and
smaller trees, favouring the small branches and twigs of the outer canopy. Certain
rainforest trees become festooned with epiphytes, others remain totally free indicating
unsuitable physical or chemical properties of the bark, including the possible presence of
toxins. Epiphytic orchids in general can also be found growing on boulders, rock outcrops
and cliff faces within the forest itself or along its margins, sometimes in quite exposed
situations.

In drier northern parts of the Australian tropics, the vegetation is exposed to harsher
conditions than on the east coast. Much of the area is covered with open woodland and
sparse grassy woodland – dry open habitats which do not support many epiphytic orchids.
In the north, these orchids are mainly found in wetter sites and areas of higher humidity
closer to the coast and on trees growing near streams, or on paperbarks in swamps and
along seepage zones. Rainforests which support epiphytes are themselves restricted to
wetter near-coastal localities or along deeper streamlines in rocky escarpments. Specialised
patches of rainforest, known as monsoonal thickets or vine thickets, also develop where
conditions are suitable. These patches of vegetation, which are often dense and can be
relatively small, are an important haven for epiphytic orchids.

The climate of these drier northern areas is strictly monsoonal, with most of the rain
falling in a relatively short, concentrated period which lasts just a few months in summer.
This period, known as the wet season (or wet), is followed by many months of winter heat

and dryness during which little or no rain falls. This period is known as the dry season (or dry). An abundance of water during the summer wet season results in hot humid conditions, the soils become sodden, and streams, even those that dry out in the winter, run freely. Plants grow rapidly in these times. New growth of the orchids is initiated by the rain that falls during the first thunderstorms that arrive at the end of the dry season and is sustained during the early part of the wet but slows and hardens as the dry season approaches. Plants stop growth completely in the dry season and many of the trees, shrubs and vines in the forests, especially in the monsoonal thickets and vine thickets, shed some, or all, of their leaves, exposing any epiphytic orchids to the hot sun. Specialised species of epiphytic orchids can survive in these monsoonal regions by coinciding their growth with the seasonal conditions, producing new shoots and roots during the summer wet and becoming dormant in the winter dry. Some species even reach their limits of survival during long, hot dry winter periods, shedding their leaves completely and their pseudobulbs shrivelling from water loss. Despite the harsh, dry conditions in winter, several species of epiphytic orchids flower at this time.

Natural hybrids

Natural hybrids, although not generally common, can occur between epiphytic orchids growing and flowering in close proximity. Natural hybrids are usually found between related species within a genus, but they can sometimes occur between species that would appear to be only distantly related. Hybrids can generally be recognised by floral features that are intermediate between the purported parents. The more abundant the parent species at any location the greater the chance of natural hybridisation taking place. Disturbances such as cyclones and land clearing can also stimulate natural hybridisation.

Epiphytic orchids and fire

Epiphytic orchids suffer drastically from fire, especially those species which form small clumps or have limited storage capacity, as in most species that have a monopodial growth habit. Intensely hot burns kill most orchids in an area and can destroy whole populations, even those growing on tall trees, cliffs and rock faces. Sometimes large clumps of bulky species with a dense, thick, root system, such as *Dockrillia striolata* and *Thelychiton speciosus*, can grow back after the fire, reviving from dormant buds that survive within the clump. The Black Summer megafires of 2019 and 2020, which impacted droughted forests from Queensland to eastern Victoria and parts of South Australia, were particularly devastating, burning more than 24 million hectares of forest and farmland. Even fern gullies and wetter forests, including rainforests, were burnt. Smaller growing epiphytic orchids were severely impacted by these fierce, hot fires which were also devastating in general for whole populations of larger lithophytic and epiphytic orchids, the extent of which is still not fully appreciated.

HABITATS

Riverine closed forest and open forest, Blencoe Falls, Qld.

Temperate moss forest, Barrington Tops, NSW.

Epiphyic orchids in lowland tropical rainforest, wet season, Moa Is., Qld.

Subtropical montane forest, Lamington NP, Qld.
J. Roberts

Subtropical rainforest, Currumbin Valley, Qld.

Escarpment rainforest in wet season, Arnhem
Land, NT.

Epacrid scrub on sand, wet season, Cape York
Pen., Qld.

Littoral rainforest in dry season, Cape York Pen., Qld.

Mangroves, Cape York Pen., Qld.

Melaleuca-dominated grassland in dry season, near Cooktown, Qld. D. Banks

Tropical paperbark grassland in wet season, Moa Is., Qld.

Rockshelf in montane tropical rainforest, Mt Lewis, Qld. D. Banks

Tropical monsoonal thicket after leaf fall, Undarra, Qld.

Rockpile vegetation, Cape York Pen., Qld.

Stunted lowland tropical rainforest and rockpiles, Dauan Island, Qld.

AUSTRALIAN
EPIPHYTIC
ORCHIDS

THE *BULBOPHYLLUM* ALLIANCE

Adelopetalum exiguum

Bulbophyllum is often treated as a very large and unwieldy genus of more than 3,000 spp. distributed in the tropical regions of Asia, SE Asia, South America and Africa. A detailed molecular phylogenetic study of Australian taxa previously placed in *Bulbophyllum* segregates them into 11 distinct genera and about 35 spp. These genera and spp. are presented here in alphabetical order.

Genus *Adelopetalum*

About 10 spp., 9 endemic in Aust.; *A. argyropus* on Norfolk Is. (page 206); an unnamed sp. on Lord Howe Is. (page 203); others in NCal, NZ. Small spp. with creeping rhizomes, thin roots and small crowded to well-spaced 1-leaved pseudobulbs. Few-flowered thread-like racemes with small flowers arise from rhizome nodes.

MAINLAND STRAND ORCHID *Adelopetalum* sp. aff. *argyropus*
Mar–May, Aug–Dec. **ID: Pseudobulbs crowded, when young with white felted bracts; flowers opening widely, yellowish/whitish, labellum yellow/orange; raceme, ovary and capsule warty.** Pseudobulbs to 8 x 6mm. Leaves to 25 x 6mm. Racemes 15–35mm. Flowers 1–4, c.3.5 x 5.5mm. **Dist.:** Qld, NSW (McPherson Ra. to Dorrigo, Yarrowitch); 600–1,000m alt. Upper branches in highland rainforest. Occas. *Exocarpos cupressiformis* in drier forest. **Status:** Highly localised, uncommon; vulnerable (Qld).

MAROON STRAND ORCHID *Adelopetalum boonjee*
Sep–Feb. **ID: Pseudobulbs few, crowded, flattened, pale green; leaves pale green, thin-textured, stiff; flowers bell-shaped, dark maroon/purple with darker striae on sepals; labellum fleshy, curved, numerous small warty bumps towards base.** Pseudobulbs to 8 x 5mm. Leaves to 40 x 4mm. Racemes 10–15mm. Flowers 2–4, c.5 x 7mm. **Dist.:** Qld (E side of Atherton Tlnd, Mt Lewis); 650–750m alt. Small tree branches in dense rainforest. **Status:** Highly localised; vulnerable.

Adelopetalum sp. aff. *argyropus*, Enfield SF, NSW. L. Copeland

Adelopetalum boonjee, Gadgarra, Qld. B. Gray

A. sp. aff. *argyropus* flowers. L. Copeland

A. boonjee, Mt Lewis, Qld. R. Tunstall

31

BLOTCHED PINEAPPLE ORCHID *Adelopetalum bracteatum*

Oct–Dec. **ID: Pseudobulbs crowded, pale green/yellowish, deeply ribbed with wrinkled ridges; racemes with conspicuous bluish bracts; flowers crowded, cream/yellowish, numerous purple or red/brown blotches; labellum pink, red, purple or yellow.** Pseudobulbs to 12 x 8mm. Leaves to 30 x 10mm. Racemes 50–100mm. Flowers 5–25, c.4 x 8mm. **Dist.:** Qld, NSW (Bunya Mtns to Dorrigo); 400–1,000m alt. Ranges and tlnds. Upper branches of rainforest trees; among lichen on shady or exposed rock faces. Plants often strongly bleached. **Status:** Locally common.

PINEAPPLE ORCHID *Adelopetalum elisae*

May–Dec. **ID: Pseudobulbs crowded, with wrinkled ridges, pale green/yellowish; flowers dominated by long narrow sepals, usually on one side of raceme, green to yellow, occas. brownish, pinkish or reddish, labellum dark red/purple.** Pseudobulbs to 30 x 20mm. Leaves to 100 x 12mm. Racemes 150–250mm. Flowers 3–12, c.20 x 15mm. **Dist.:** Qld, NSW (Bunya Mtns to Blue Mtns); 400–1,200m alt. Drier humid forests in hilly/mountainous areas inland from coast; buoyant airy ridges in rainforest; shady or exposed rock faces. **Status:** Widespread, sporadic.

TINY STRAND ORCHID *Adelopetalum exiguum*

Feb–Jun. **ID: Pseudobulbs widely spaced, grooved; leaves dark green, glossy; flowers small, greenish/cream, labellum yellow.** Pseudobulbs to 10 x 8mm. Leaves to 50 x 9mm. Racemes 40–90mm. Flowers 1–5, c.6 x 10mm. **Dist.:** Qld, NSW (Maleny to Mumbulla Mtn); 5–1,200m alt. Coast to ranges. Mainly wetter forests on trees, rocks and cliff faces; near streams in drier humid forest. Mainly grows in shade, occas. exposed. Often extensive patches on boulders. Occas. on Antarctic Beech. **Status:** Widespread, common.

SMOOTH STRAND ORCHID *Adelopetalum lageniforme*

Nov–Feb. **ID: Pseudobulbs spaced, flattish, pale green, deeply grooved; leaves dark green, stiff; flowers bell-shaped, white, cream or pale green with darker stripes, labellum pink (flowers rarely wholly pale pink).** Pseudobulbs to 10 x 10mm. Leaves to 100 x 8mm. Racemes 40–70mm. Flowers 1–4, c.7 x 5mm. **Dist.:** Qld (Mt Finnigan to Koombooloomba); 900–1,600m alt. Shrubs, trees and rocks on buoyant, airy/misty/foggy ridges in moderate/high alt. rainforest. **Status:** Locally common.

Adelopetalum bracteatum, Whian Whian, NSW. D. Banks   *A. bracteatum*, Mann R., NSW. L. Copeland

Adelopetalum elisae, Warra NP, NSW. L. Copeland   *A. elisae*, Cathedral Rocks, NSW. D. Banks

A. exiguum, Gara Gorge, NSW. L. Copeland   *A. exiguum*, Werrikimbe NP, NSW. L. Copeland

Adelopetalum lageniforme, Tinaroo Hills, Qld. D. Banks   *A. lageniforme*, Tinaroo Hills, Qld. E. Rotherham

WARTY STRAND ORCHID *Adelopetalum lilianiae*

Jul–Sep. **ID: Pseudobulbs very widely spaced, deeply grooved; leaves green/yellowish; flowers bell-shaped, cream, pale green or reddish with dark red stripes and pink labellum; sepals sparsely warty.** Pseudobulbs to 12 x 3mm. Leaves to 25 x 8mm. Racemes 15–25mm. Flowers 1–3, c.5 x 8mm. **Dist.:** Qld (Big Tlnd to Evelyn Tlnd); 900–1,600m alt. Shrubs, trees and rocks on buoyant airy/misty/foggy ridges in moist/wet high alt. rainforest; twigs and upper branches of tall rainforest trees. **Status:** Locally common.

CUPPED STRAND ORCHID *Adelopetalum newportii*

Sep–Dec. **ID: Pseudobulbs widely spaced, grooved or ribbed; leaves dark green; flowers bell-shaped, white, cream or greenish, rarely pink, dorsal sepal and petals occas. with red stripes; labellum sparsely hairy.** Pseudobulbs to 15 x 12mm. Leaves to 70 x 12mm. Racemes 50–90mm. Flowers 1–8, c.6 x 5mm. **Dist.:** Qld (McIlwraith Ra., Big Tlnd to Eungella); 600–1,200m alt. Trees and rocks in rainforest and humid open forest with buoyant air movement. **Status:** Widespread, common.

BLOTCHED WAX ORCHID *Adelopetalum weinthalii* subsp. *weinthalii*

Mar–May. **ID: Pseudobulbs crowded, wrinkled, when young with white felted bracts; leaves dark green; flower waxy, white, cream or greenish with red/purplish spots, blotches and suffusions, labellum mostly red/purple.** Pseudobulbs to 20 x 14mm. Leaves to 30 x 9mm. Racemes short. Flower single, c.7 x 20mm. **Dist.:** Qld, NSW (Bunya Mtns to Dorrigo); 600–1,200m alt. Scaly bark of upper branches of large Hoop Pines where fogs and mists are frequent. **Status:** Highly localised, sporadic.

STREAKED WAX ORCHID *Adelopetalum weinthalii* subsp. *striatum*

Mar–Jun. **ID: Northern variant that differs from typical subspecies by slightly larger flowers with broader, distinctly striate segements (rather than spotted/blotched).** **Dist.:** Qld (Dawes Ra., Kroombit Tops); 650–930m alt. Occurs c.300km N of populations of typical subspecies, growing on large hoop pines on higher parts of ranges. **Status:** Highly localised.

Adelopetalum lilianae, Ravenshoe, Qld. B. Gray

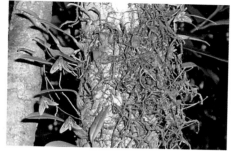

A. lilianiae, Mt Lewis, Qld. J. Mohandas

Adelopetalum newportii, Mt Windsor Tlnd, Qld. D. Banks

A. newportii, Eungella, Qld. D. Banks

Adelopetalum weinthalii subsp. *weinthalii*, Dorrigo, NSW. D. Banks

Adelopetalum weinthalii subsp. *weinthalii*, Dorrigo, NSW. L. Copeland

Adelopetalum weinthalii subsp. *striatum*, Kroombit Tops, Qld. D. Banks

A. weinthalii subsp. *striatum*, Kroombit Tops, Qld. R. Tunstall

Genus *Blepharochilum*

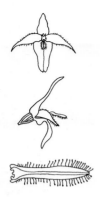

About 45 spp., 2 endemic in Aust.; others in Indon., Vanuatu, PNG, NCal. Densely crowded, matting orchids with thin roots, creeping rhizomes, small, crowded pseudobulbs with a single fleshy channelled leaf and single small dark-coloured flower arising from base of pseudobulb. Labellum trembling in a breeze, margins with long fine hairs.

Blepharochilum macphersonii

SMALL EYELASH ORCHID *Blepharochilum macphersonii*
Mar–Aug. **ID: Pseudobulbs dark green; leaves thick, fleshy, dark green, deeply channelled; racemes filiform; flowers dark red/purple, rarely pink, green or white; labellum narrow throughout.** Pseudobulbs c.2 x 1mm. Leaves to 25 x 4mm. Racemes 12–40mm. Flowers 8–12 x 8–12mm. **Dist.:** Qld (Big Tlnd to Rockhampton); 5–1,400m alt. Trees, rocks, boulders and cliff faces in rainforest and sheltered areas of humid open forest; occas. mangroves. Variable leaf shape. **Status:** Widespread, common.

HERMON'S EYELASH ORCHID *Blepharochilum sladeanum*
Mar–Aug. **ID: Differs from previous sp. by longer leaves, racemes often curved and larger flowers with labellum widening towards apex.** Leaves to 30 x 6mm. Racemes 50–70mm. Flowers 15–25 x 15–25mm. **Dist.:** Qld (Atherton Tlnd, higher peaks between Mossman and Mt Bartle Frere); 800–1,300m alt. Shrubs, smaller branches and twigs of high alt. rainforest trees where fogs and mists are frequent. Not always easy to distinguish from previous sp. **Status:** Highly localised.

Blepharochilum sladeanum

Blepharochilum macphersonii, Mt Baldy, Qld. D. Banks

B. macphersonii, Eungella, Qld. D. Banks

Blepharochilum sladeanum, Mt Hypipamee, Qld. D. Banks

B. sladeanum, The Crater, Qld. B. Gray

Genus *Cirrhopetalum*

Distinctive genus of c.75 spp. distributed from Africa to Asia and the Pacific. Two spp. extending to Aust. Mainly recognised by the longer-than-wide flowers being grouped together in a spreading semicircular umbel-like pattern at the end of a long flower stem. Additional features include a 1-leaved pseudobulb, dorsal sepal with an apical thread-like filament and lateral sepals fused on both sides to base of column foot and then twisted once to bring their outer margins together where they are fused to form a convex blade. NOTES: Flowers last several days.

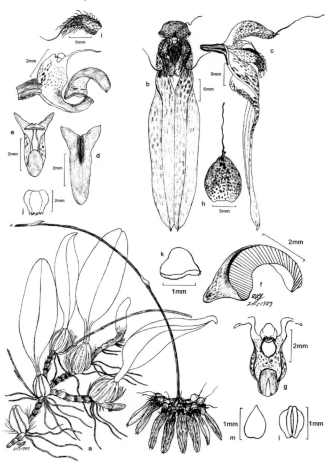

Cirrhopetalum clavigerum, Leo Ck, Qld. a. flowering plant; b. flower from front; c. flower from side; d. labellum from above, flattened; e. labellum from below; f. longitudinal section of labellum; g. column from front; h. dorsal sepal; i. petal; j. anther cap from above; k. anther cap from side; l. pollinarium; m. pollinium.

PALE UMBRELLA ORCHID *Cirrhopetalum clavigerum*

(Oct–) Jan–Mar. **ID: Pseudobulbs grooved, dark green; leaves dark green, fleshy; flowers greenish/cream to yellowish or pinkish, with fine purple spots, labellum dark purple; petal margins with long thin hairs.** Pseudobulbs to 45 x 20mm. Leaves to 150 x 30mm. Flower stems to 200mm. Flowers 5–10, c.40 x 5mm. **Dist.:** Qld (CYP – Iron Ra., McIlwraith Ra.); 300–500m alt.; also PNG, NCal. Trees, vines and rocks on ridgetops, steep slopes and beside streams in rainforest. **Status:** Highly localised; vulnerable.

Cirrhopetalum clavigerum, Leo Ck, Qld. B. Gray

Bulbophyllum clavigerum, Leo Ck, Qld. M. Harrison

WISPY UMBRELLA ORCHID *Cirrhopetalum gracillimum*

Aug–Mar. **ID: Pseudobulbs dark green, 4–5 prominent ridges; leaves dark green, thick, leathery; flowers purplish/red with white/cream labellum; dorsal sepal and petal margins hairy; sepals ending in long thread-like tails.** Pseudobulbs to 18 x 5mm. Leaves to 80 x 35mm. Flower stems to 250mm. Flowers 6–10, c.50 x 8mm. **Dist.:** Qld (CYP – Janet Ra., Iron Ra., Tozer Ra.); 300–400m alt.; also PNG, NCal., Asia. Trees on ridges and slopes in stunted rainforest and beside streams. **Status:** Highly localised; vulnerable.

Cirrhopetalum gracillimum, Tozer Ra., Qld. D. Banks

C. gracillimum, Captain Billy Ck, Qld. R. Tunstall

Genus *Ephippium*

Ephippium ciliatum

About 20 spp., 1 extending to Aust.; others in Pacific Is. Creeping rhizomes appressed to host, well-spaced 1-leaved pseudobulbs, leaf large and 1-flowered raceme arising from a rhizome node. Sepals with long thread-like tips, sometimes clubbed. NOTES: Flowers short-lasting.

RED HORNTAIL ORCHID *Ephippium ciliatum*

Jul–Oct. **ID: Pseudobulbs tapered, grooved; flowers red/purplish with yellow/white margins; dorsal sepal densely hairy; lateral sepals fused at base with long tangling thread-like tails; labellum tip trunk-like.** Pseudobulbs to 40 x 12mm. Leaf and petiole to 150 x 25mm. Racemes 100–200mm. Flowers to 90 x 25mm. **Dist.:** Qld (Moa Is., CYP–Shelburne Bay, Rocky R.); 20–150m alt.; also PNG. Trunks and larger branches of fibrous-barked trees and palms on rainforest margins, vine forest and monsoonal thickets. **Status:** Locally common.

Genus *Fruticicola*

Fruticicola radicans

About 25 spp., 1 endemic in Aust.; others in PNG. Pendulous/dangling sparsely branched stems covered with papery bracts, attached by basal roots only, small pseudobulbs with relatively large leaf and short 1-flowered racemes arising singly from rhizome node. Flowers small, often striped, petals small and labellum underside hairy. NOTES: Flowers last 1–2 days.

STRIPED PYJAMA ORCHID *Fruticicola radicans*

Sporadic. **ID: Pseudobulbs partially hidden; leaves bright green, shiny, shallowly channelled, often curved; flowers pink, cream or yellow with red/purple stripes (rarely unstriped), labellum red and yellow/orange.** Stems 100–400mm. Pseudobulbs to 15 x 3mm. Leaves to 80 x 18mm. Racemes 6–10mm. Flowers c.4 x 5mm. **Dist.:** Qld (Mt Finnigan to Yeppoon); 5–1,200m alt. Coast to ranges and tlnds on trees, boulders and cliffs in or close to rainforest and humid slopes near streams. **Status:** Widespread, common.

Ephippium ciliatum, Moa Is., Qld. D. Jones

E. ciliatum, Heathlands, Qld. M. Harrison

Fruticicola radicans, Mossman Gorge, Qld. D. Banks

F. radicans, Mt Finnigan, Qld. D. Banks

41

Genus *Kaurorchis*

About 5 spp., 1 endemic in Aust.; others in PNG, NCal. Brittle creeping rhizomes appressed closely to host, thin spreading roots, tiny widely spaced pseudobulbs with proportionately large fleshy leaf, relatively long flower stem arising from rhizome node, wers last few days.

CREEPING BRITTLE ORCHID
Kaurorchis evasa

Nov–Mar. **ID: Long slender strands covered with brown bracts, inconspicuous pseudobulbs, dark green leaves and erect thin racemes (widening near apex) carrying a dense head of pink/reddish flowers with dark red stripes and yellow tips.** Pseudobulbs to 7 x 4mm. Leaves to 35 x 30mm. Racemes 60–100mm. Flowers 10–25, c.3mm across. **Dist.:** Qld (Mt Finnigan to Mt Spec); 800–1,600m alt. Trees, shrubs, mossy boulders and rocks in highland rainforest with winds, clouds and frequent mists. **Status:** Locally common.

Kaurorchis evasa

Kaurorchis evasa, Tinaroo Hills, Qld. D. Jones

K. evasa, Tinaroo Hills, Qld. D. Jones

Genus *Oncophyllum*

Three spp., 2 endemic in Aust., 1 in NCal. Small moss-like orchids clumping or spreading by thin strands with short stubby unbranched roots, tiny crowded rounded pseudobulbs each with a tiny scale-like leaf that is shed after few months and thread-like 1-flowered racemes arising from base of pseudobulb. Flowers small, cupped. Ovaries minutely warty. NOTES: Easily overlooked and misidentified as a moss or lichen. Flowers last several days. Pseudobulbs hollow with internal cavity that contains stomata. Only 2 roots per pseudobulb.

Oncophyllum minutissimum

GREEN BEAD ORCHID *Oncophyllum globuliforme Sep–Nov, May–Aug.* **ID: Pseudobulbs globe-like, pale green; leaf scale-like; ovary irregularly corrugated; flowers cream with yellow labellum (rarely red with cream labellum).** Pseudobulbs 1–2mm across. Leaves 1–1.5mm long. Racemes 10–15mm. Flowers 3–4mm across. **Dist.:** Qld, NSW (Paluma to Bonalbo); 300–900m alt. Scaly bark on the higher parts of trunk and larger branches of Hoop Pines. Often on fallen branches. **Status:** Highly localised; vulnerable.

Oncophyllum globuliforme, Kroombit Tops, Qld. D. Banks   *O. globuliforme*, Lamington NP, Qld. R. Tunstall

RED BEAD ORCHID *Oncophyllum minutissimum*

Oct–Feb. **ID: Pseudobulbs round, flattened, green to reddish; leaf scale-like, curved; ovary hairy; flowers whitish to reddish with broad dark red stripes and red labellum.** Pseudobulbs 2–3mm across. Leaves c.1mm long. Racemes c.3mm. Flowers 3–3.5mm across. **Dist.:** Qld, NSW (Blackdown Tlnd to Milton); 5–500m alt. Coast to inland ranges and gorges in shade or sun; trees, boulders and cliff faces near stream banks, coastal scrub, littoral rainforest, swamps, mangroves; large relict fig trees in paddocks and suburbia. Pseudobulbs deep red/purple in strong light. **Status:** Widespread, common.

Oncophyllum minutissimum, Iluka, NSW. L. Copeland   *O. minutissimum*, Iluka NR, NSW. L. Copeland

Genus *Oxysepala*

About 25 spp., 8 endemic in Aust.; others in SE Asia and Pacific. Stems creeping or pendulous, covered with papery bracts, roots thin from basal nodes or along rhizomes, small widely spaced pseudobulbs each with a sessile or petiolate fleshy grooved leaf and 1-flowered racemes arising singly or in groups among bracts at nodes. Flowers small, colourful, with thick fleshy segments, arising at intervals from floral meristems in rhizome nodes. NOTES: Flowers often don't open widely, last few days.

Oxysepala schilleriana

TANGLED ROPE ORCHID *Oxysepala gadgarrensis*

Jul–Sep. **ID: Stems pendulous, freely branching, attached by basal roots, covered by purple/brown bracts; pseudobulbs hidden by bracts; flower usually single, cream/white with orange/yellow tips.** Stems 100–200mm. Pseudobulbs to 6 x 1.5mm. Leaf and petiole to 30 x 4mm. Flowers c.6 x 5mm. **Dist.:** Qld (Big Tlnd to Koombooloomba); 600–1,400m alt. Mossy trunks and branches in rainforest with buoyant air movement, frequent clouds and mists; relict trees in paddocks. **Status:** Locally common.

Oxysepala gadgarrensis, Tinaroo Hills, Qld. D. Jones

O. gadgarrensis, Mt Lewis, Qld. D. Banks

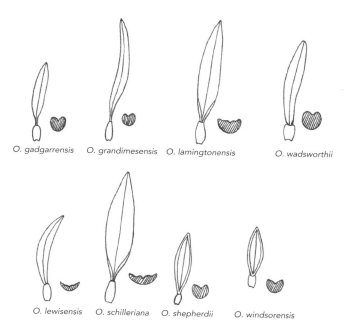

Oxysepala spp., leaf, pseudobulb and pseudobulb cross-section.

PALE ROPE ORCHID *Oxysepala grandimesensis*

May–Jun. **ID:** Stems suberect to pendulous, sparsely branched, attached by basal roots, bracts brown; pseudobulbs exposed; leaves dark green, narrowly and shallowly grooved; flower usually single, fleshy, white; sepals with white/yellowish thread-like tips. Stems 20–80mm. Pseudobulbs to 6 x 2.5mm. Leaf and petiole to 50 x 5mm. Flowers c.8 x 7mm. **Dist.:** Qld (Big Tlnd); 600–800m alt. Small upper branches of rainforest trees. **Status:** Highly localised; vulnerable.

CREAM ROPE ORCHID *Oxysepala lamingtonensis*

Sep–Nov. **ID:** Stems pendulous, unbranched/sparsely branched, bracts brown; pseudobulbs exposed, green; leaf sessile, broadly and shallowly grooved; flower single, cream/white with yellow tips or wholly yellowish, labellum red/brown or orange. Stems 100–200mm. Pseudobulbs to 12 x 3.5mm. Leaves to 80 x 14mm. Flowers c.9.5 x 4mm. **Dist.:** Qld, NSW (McPherson Ra. to Woodenbong); 800–1,200m alt. Small trees and rocks in rainforest close to rocky escarpments; also rainforest margins. **Status:** Highly localised. **See also:** *O. shepherdii*.

MT LEWIS ROPE ORCHID *Oxysepala lewisensis*

Aug–Oct. **ID:** Stems semi-pendulous, sparsely branched, attached by basal roots, bracts pale brown; pseudobulbs exposed, green; leaf and petiole dark green, broadly grooved; flower single, white. Stems 60–150mm. Pseudobulbs to 5 x 3.5mm. Leaf and petiole to 22 x 5mm. Flowers c.5 x 4mm. **Dist.:** Qld (Mt Lewis, Carbine Tlnd, Mt Windsor Tlnd); 1,000–1,250m alt. Upper branches of trees on buoyant airy/misty ridge tops in highland rainforest. **Status:** Highly localised.

RED ROPE ORCHID *Oxysepala schilleriana* subsp. *schilleriana*

Mar–Aug. **ID:** Stems pendulous, sparsely branched, attached by basal roots; pseudobulbs yellow to green, partly hidden by greyish bracts; leaf sessile, fleshy, variable in size, shape, thickness, grooving and colour; flowers in clusters, waxy, red/orange with pale centre, labellum red/brown, hairy. Stems 100–300mm. Pseudobulbs to 6 x 4mm. Leaves to 100 x 25mm. Flowers c.7 x 3mm. **Dist.:** Qld, NSW (Mt Finnigan to Bulahdelah); 5–1,250m alt. Coast to ranges and tlnds. Shrubs, trees and rocks in rainforest, stream banks and swamps. **Status:** Widespread, locally common.

Oxysepala grandimesensis, Big Tlnd, Qld. D. Banks   *O. grandimesensis*, Big Tlnd, Qld. D. Jones

Oxysepala lamingtonensis, Lamington NP, Qld. L. Copeland   *O. lamingtonensis*, Lamington NP, Qld. L. Copeland

Oxysepala lewisensis, Mt Lewis, Qld. D. Banks   *O. lewisensis*, Mt Lewis, Qld. D. Banks

O. schilleriana subsp. *schilleriana*, Mt Lewis, Qld. D. Banks   *O. s.* subsp. *schilleriana*, Mt Baldy, Qld. D. Banks

MANGROVE ROPE ORCHID *Oxysepala schilleriana* subsp. *maritima*
Apr–Aug. **ID: Differs from previous subsp. by its thinner-textured leaves, smaller paler flowers and less hairy labellum. Dist.:** Qld (Cairns to Hinchinbrook Is.); 0–20m alt. Mangroves and trees lining estuaries and lowland swamps. **Status:** Localised.

WHEAT LEAF ORCHID *Oxysepala shepherdii*
Mar–Nov. **ID: Stems appressed to host, branching freely, roots from most nodes; pseudobulbs tiny, exposed, flattish; leaf sessile, fleshy, green, deeply and broadly grooved; flower single, white/cream with yellowish tips, labellum orange to red/brown.** Pseudobulbs to 3 x 4mm. Leaves to 40 x 8mm. Flowers c.5 x 3mm. **Dist.:** Qld, NSW (Nambour to Mumbulla Mtn); 5–1,000m alt. Trees, shrubs and rocks in rainforest close to permanent streams; sheltered gorges and moist humid areas of open forest; trees in swamps. **Status:** Widespread, common. **See also:** *O. lamingtonensis.*

YELLOW ROPE ORCHID *Oxysepala wadsworthii*
Sep–Nov. **ID: Stems pendulous, sparsely branched, attached by basal roots; pseudobulbs partly hidden by brown bracts; leaf sessile, dark green, narrowly and shallowly grooved; flowers cream or pale green with brown/orange labellum.** Stems 50–250mm. Pseudobulbs to 30 x 20mm. Leaves to 60 x 8mm. Flowers 1–3, c.6 x 6mm. **Dist.:** Qld (Big Tlnd to Mt Spec); 700–1,600m alt. Rainforest trees on airy/misty/foggy ridge tops; relict trees in paddocks. **Status:** Locally common.

THREAD-TIPPED ROPE ORCHID *Oxysepala windsorensis*
May–Aug. **ID: Stems pendulous, sparsely branched, attached by basal roots; pseudobulbs partly hidden by brown bracts; leaf sessile, dark green, fleshy, broadly and deeply grooved; flowers cream to greenish-cream; sepal tips long, thread-like.** Stems 100–300mm. Pseudobulbs to 8 x 5mm. Leaves to 30 x 6mm. Flowers 1–2, c.15 x 15mm. **Dist.:** Qld (Mt Windsor Tlnd, Mt Lewis); 1,000–1,250m alt. Upper branches of trees on airy/misty/foggy ridge tops in high alt. rainforest. **Status:** Highly localised.

Oxysepala schilleriana subsp. *maritima*,
Russell R., Qld. R. Tunstall

Oxysepala shepherdii, Cottan-Bimbang NP, NSW. L. Copeland

O. shepherdii, Nowra, NSW. D. Banks

Oxysepala wadsworthii, Mt Baldy, Qld. D. Banks

O. wadsworthii, Mt Baldy, Qld. D. Banks

Oxysepala windsorensis, Mt Lewis, Qld. M. Harrison

O. windsorensis, Mt Windsor Tlnd, Qld. D. Jones

Genus *Papulipetalum*

About 10 spp., 1 endemic in Aust.; others in PNG. Crowded, flask-shaped pseudobulbs, when young covered with soft fibrous sheaths, each with a large fleshy leaf attached by a long fleshy basally jointed petiole and 1-flowered racemes arising from base of a pseudobulb. Flowers nodding, with broad sepals and small petals. NOTES: Flowers last few days.

Papulipetalum nematopodum

GREEN COWL ORCHID

Papulipetalum nematopodum

Sep–Nov. **ID: Pseudobulbs crowded, flask-shaped with narrow extended neck; leaf shiny, dark green; flower stem fleshy, apex sharply curved; flower nodding, cream or pale green with few red spots, labellum pink/red; petals with purple apical spot.** Pseudobulbs to 20 x 9mm. Leaves to 130 x 20mm. Flower stems 50–70mm. Flowers 10–12mm across. **Dist.:** Qld (Big Tlnd to Mt Elliot); 400–1,200m alt. Trees, shrubs and rocks on buoyant airy/misty ridges in rainforest. **Status:** Locally common.

Papulipetalum nematopodum, The Crater, Qld. D. Banks

P. nematopodum, The Crater, Qld. D. Banks

Genus *Serpenticaulis*

Serpenticaulis bowkettiae

About 5 spp., 4 endemic in Aust., another in NCal. Epiphytic orchids forming extended strands or sparse clumps with thin creeping rhizomes appressed to host, short roots arising from nodes, small widely spaced pseudobulbs appressed to rhizome each with a single relatively small leathery leaf and 1-flowered thread-like racemes arising from rhizome nodes. NOTES: Flowers nodding, lasting 1–2 days, produced in sporadic bursts throughout year.

STRIPED SNAKE ORCHID *Serpenticaulis bowkettiae* *Apr–Sep.* **ID: Pseudobulbs flattish, deeply grooved; leaf dark green, notched; flower nodding, cream with red stripes, occas. wholly reddish; labellum reddish.** Pseudobulbs to 10 x 5mm. Leaves to 25 x 12mm. Racemes 6–12mm. Flowers c.7 x 8mm. **Dist.:** Qld (McIlwraith Ra., Big Tlnd to Tully R.); commonly 600–1,200m alt. but also coastal lowlands S of Innisfail. Trees, rocks and boulders in moist/wet rainforest and open forest in ranges and tlnds. **Status:** Locally common. **See also:** *S. wolfei.*

Sepenticaulis bowkettiae, Herberton, Qld. D. Banks

S. bowkettiae, Tinaroo Hills, Qld. D. Banks

51

COMMON SNAKE ORCHID *Serpenticaulis johnsonii*

Sporadic **ID: Pseudobulbs flattened, grooved, green, reddish or purplish; leaf dark green; flower horizontal, red, brown, green or yellowish with red lines; labellum base dark red, apex yellow.** Pseudobulbs to 18 x 15mm. Leaves to 70 x 20mm. Racemes 20–30mm. Flowers c.10 x 20mm. **Dist.:** Qld (Big Tlnd to Paluma); 200–1,400m alt. Shrubs, trees and boulders in rainforest and humid open forest; relict trees in paddocks. **Status:** Widespread, locally common. **See also:** *S. whitei.*

YELLOW SNAKE ORCHID *Serpenticaulis whitei*

Sporadic **ID: Pseudobulbs flattened, grooved, green, reddish or purplish; leaf dark green; flower horizontal, bright yellow or orange; labellum base red, apex yellow.** Pseudobulbs to 18 x 15mm. Leaves to 40 x 15mm. Racemes 20–30mm. Flowers c.7 x 15mm. **Dist.:** Qld (mainly Atherton and Evelyn Tlnd; also Mossman to Daintree); 20–1,400m alt. Shrubs and trees in rainforest and humid open forest. **Status:** Locally common. **See also:** *S. johnsonii.*

FLESHY SNAKE ORCHID *Serpenticaulis wolfei*

Apr–Sep. **ID: Pseudobulbs flattened, faintly grooved; leaf dark green, thick, fleshy; flower nodding, cream with dark red stripes; labellum reddish with yellow tip.** Pseudobulbs to 9 x 5mm. Leaves to 25 x 6mm. Racemes 2–3mm. Flowers c.8 x 8mm. **Dist.:** Qld (Carbine Tlnd to Mt Windsor Tlnd); 900–1,200m alt. Upper branches of rainforest trees at moderate to high alt. Notable for its thick fleshy leaves. **Status:** Highly localised; rare. **See also:** *S. bowkettae.*

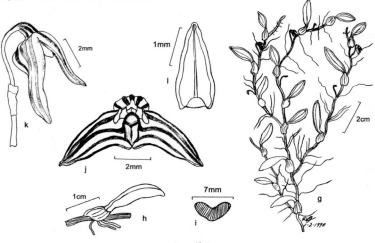

S. wolfei.

Serpenticaulis johnsonii, Mt Lewis, Qld. D. Banks

S. johnsonii, Mt Windsor Tlnd, Qld. D. Banks

Serpenticaulis whitei, Mt Windsor Tlnd, Qld. D. Banks

S. whitei, Herberton Ra., Qld. R. Tunstall

Serpenticaulis wolfei, Mt Windsor Tlnd, Qld. B. Gray

Genus *Sestochilos*

About 45 spp., 1 extending to Aust.; others in Asia and Pacific. Epiphytic orchids forming extended strands or spreading clumps with creeping rhizomes covered with papery bracts that break into fibres, pseudobulbs curved forwards along rhizome then erect, each with a single large fleshy leaf and 1-flowered racemes (rarely 2–3-flowered) arising from rhizome nodes, the peduncle with stem-clasping tubular bracts. NOTES: Flowers relatively large, upward-facing, strongly fragrant, lasting 1–3 days. Labellum trembling in a breeze.

FRUIT-FLY ORCHID *Sestochilos baileyi*

Oct–Feb.; also sporadic **ID: Pseudobulbs curved; leaf pale green/yellowish; racemes erect; flower upward-facing, creamy-yellow with red/purple spots (rarely white or yellow and unspotted), ageing pink, fruity scent.** Pseudobulbs to 30 x 15mm. Leaves to 300 x 90mm. Racemes 60–100mm. Flowers c.25 x 40mm. **Dist.:** Qld (Moa Is., Cape York to Paluma Ra.); 5–1,200m alt.; also PNG, Irian Jaya. Coast to ranges, tlnds and W slopes of Dividing Ra. in open forest, rainforest, mangroves. Shade or sun. Flowers partially close at night. **Status:** Widespread, common.

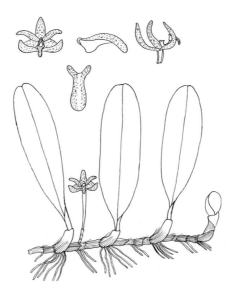

Sestochilos baileyi

Sestochilos baileyi, Mossman Gorge, Qld. D. Titmuss

THE *DENDROBIUM* ALLIANCE

A group of spp. that have been loosely placed in the genus *Dendrobium* but which detailed molecular-based studies show as being better treated in segregate genera within 3 major subtribes, Dendrobiinae and Grastidiinae and Epigeneiinae. The *Dendrobium* alliance in Australia consists of 26 genera, 3 in subtribe Dendrobiinae and 23 in tribe Grastidiinae (none in Epigeneiinae). Overall in Aust. the *Dendrobium* alliance consists of c.95 spp., the majority endemic. The genera and spp. are presented here in alphabetical order within each subtribe.

TRIBE DENDROBIEAE, SUBTRIBE DENDROBIINAE

Genus *Ceraia*

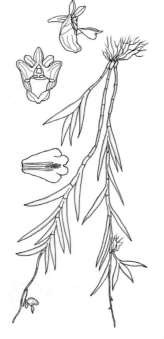

Ceraia macfarlanei

About 55 spp, 1 widespread sp., *C. saaronica*, on Christmas Is. (page 214) and *C. macfarlanei* on Dauan Is. in Torres Strait; others in Asia and Pacific. Straggly/untidy epiphytic or lithophytic orchids with differing growth features. Both native spp. share the habit of leaves being arranged in 2 rows and a leafless apical section where the flowers are borne. The short-lived flowers arise singly at sporadic intervals from long-lived nodes.

SHAGGY ORCHID *Ceraia macfarlanei*
Sporadic flowerer. **ID: Pseudobulbs pale, narrow upper leafy section flattened; leaves laterally flattened, sharply pointed; flowers pale greenish/cream with red stripes; labellum green and white.** Pseudobulbs to 60 x 1cm. Leaves to 60 x 8mm. Flower c.15 x 12mm. **Dist.:** Qld (Dauan Is., Torres Strait); 0–50m alt.; also PNG. Trees and rocks in stunted rainforest and beach scrub. Flowers arise sporadically and last 3–4 days. Reproduces freely by aerial growths. **Status:** Highly localised in Aust.; locally common on Dauan Is.

Ceraia macfarlanei, Dauan Is., Qld. B. Lavarack

C. macfarlanei, Dauan Is, Qld. B. Lavarack

Ceraia macfarlanei, Dauan Is., Qld. R. Tunstall

Ceraia macfarlanei showing pseudobulbs with apical growths and folded leaves sheathing at the base. D. Jones

Genus *Coelandria*

BOTTLEBRUSH ORCHID *Coelandria smillieae*
Aug–Nov. **ID:** Single sp. that extends to Aust.
Pseudobulbs leafy for first year then bare, spindle-shaped, green/yellow with dark nodal rings; leaves bright green, often twisted; racemes erect, bottlebrush-like; flowers semi-tubular, densely crowded, cream or pink, labellum apex dark green. Pseudobulbs to 1m x 3cm. Leaves to 20 x 4cm. Racemes 80–150mm. Flowers c.25 x 18mm. **Dist.:** Qld (Torres Strait Is., Cape York to Townsville); 5–700m alt.; also PNG, Indon. Coastal lowlands to ranges on rocks and trees in various humid habitats; palms and trees in swamps. **Status:** Widespread, common.

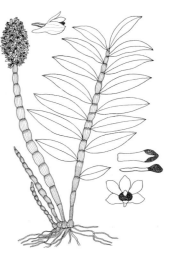

Coelandria smillieae

Coelandria smillieae, Carron Valley, Qld. D. Jones

C. smillieae, Daintree, Qld. M. Clements

Genus *Dendrobium*

About 50 spp., 1 widespread sp. extending to Aust.; others in Asia, SE Asia and Pacific. Species of true *Dendrobium* can be recognised by the following features. Epiphytic/lithophytic orchids with long narrow cylindrical pseudobulbs. Leaves present in first year, shedding as pseudobulb matures. Racemes short, arising from lateral nodes, never from terminal nodes. Flowers often colourful, the labellum unlobed, with hairy margins and papillate surface.

FRINGED TREE ORCHID *Dendrobium macrostachyum*

Dendrobium macrostachyum

Dec–Mar. **ID: Pseudobulbs pendulous, somewhat zigzagged; leaves thin-textured, pale green; flowers whitish/green, ageing yellow; labellum whitish with red/mauve veins and 3 hairy ridges, margins hairy, incurved to widely spreading.** Pseudobulbs to 600 x 5mm. Leaves to 80 x 25mm. Racemes 15–25mm. Flowers 1–3, 15–20mm across.

Dist.: Qld (CYP – Bamaga to McIlwraith Ra.); 50–350m alt.; also Asia, Pacific. Low to moderate alt. in rainforest and monsoonal thickets where trees shed leaves in dry season. Flowers self-pollinating, often opening tardily, if at all. **Status:** Localised.

Dendrobium macrostachyum, Claudie Scrub, Qld. R. Tunstall

Dendrobium macrostachyum fruit, Claudie R., Qld. D. Jones

Dendrobium macrostachyum, Iron Ra., Qld. R. Tunstall

TRIBE DENDROBIEAE, SUBTRIBE GRASTIDIINAE

Genus *Australorchis*

Four spp. all endemic in Aust. Epiphytic orchids with short swollen conical pseudobulbs, 1–2(–3) narrow thin leaves terminal on pseudobulbs and multiflowered racemes arising in upper leaf axils.

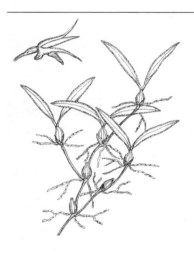

Australorchis carrii

FURROWED MOON ORCHID
Australorchis carrii

Aug–Oct. **ID: Long strands or branching tangled masses, roots often stilt-like; pseudobulbs widely spaced, yellow/green, furrowed; leaves dark green; flowers white/cream with narrow pointed tepals; labellum orange/yellow.** Pseudobulbs to 35 x 15mm. Leaves to 100 x 10mm. Racemes 30–80mm. Flowers 5–10, 8–10mm across. **Dist.:** Qld (Mt Finnigan to Koombooloomba); 500–1,600m alt. Exposed branches of tall rainforest trees, often on ridgelines where fogs, mists and clouds are frequent. **Status:** Locally common.

Australorchis carrii, Mt Baldy, Qld. D. Banks

A. carrii, Mt Lewis, Qld. R. Tunstall

A. carrii, Mt Haig, Qld. M. Clements

EUNGELLA MOON ORCHID *Australorchis eungellensis*

Feb–Apr. **ID: Compact clumps; pseudobulbs crowded, covered by brown sheaths when young, conical, furrowed, often yellowish; leaves 2, oblong, dark green; racemes long, thin, arching/drooping; flowers cream/whitish to green/yellow, waxy, cupped, labellum orange.** Pseudobulbs to 40 x 20mm. Leaves to 100 x 13mm. Racemes 150–250mm. Flowers 20–35, 10–12mm across. **Dist.:** Qld (Clarke Ra., Eungella Ra.); 400–1,000m alt. Ironbarks in open forest; trees on rainforest margins, usually in bright light. **Status:** Highly localised; locally common.

Australorchis monophylla

LILY-OF-THE-VALLEY ORCHID *Australorchis monophylla*

Aug–Dec. **ID: Strands or spreading branching clumps; pseudobulbs conical, furrowed, often yellow; leaves terminal, 1–2, bright green, thin-textured but tough; flowers scented, bell-shaped, yellow, waxy.** Pseudobulbs to 120 x 30mm. Leaves to 120 x 25mm. Racemes 150–250mm. Flowers 5–20, 6–8mm across. **Dist.:** Qld, NSW (Big Tlnd to Grafton); 50–1,000m alt. Coast to ranges and tlnds. Rocks, boulders, cliff faces and trees in humid forests and drier rainforest; upper branches of tall rainforest trees **Status:** Widespread, common.

SMALL MOON ORCHID *Australorchis schneiderae*

Jan–Apr. **ID: Compact clumps; pseudobulbs crowded, furrowed, often yellowish; leaves 2, dark green, often twisted at base; flowers cream/whitish to green/yellow (rarely pinkish), waxy, cupped.** Pseudobulbs to 25 x 15mm. Leaves to 70 x 8mm. Racemes 80–170mm. Flowers 5–25, 7–9mm across. **Dist.:** Qld, NSW (Gympie to Kyogle); 100–1,500m alt. Upper branches of rainforest trees, particularly Hoop Pines, in humid airy situations in bright light; occas. rocks and cliff faces. Mainly high alt. **Status:** Highly localised.

Australorchis eungellensis, Eungella, Qld. D. Banks

A. eungellensis, Eungella, Qld. G. Leafberg

Australorchis monophylla, Pine Brush SF, NSW. L. Copeland

A. monophylla, Pine Brush SF, NSW. L. Copeland

A. schneiderae, Richmond Ra. NP, NSW. L. Copeland

A. schneiderae, Richmond Ra. NP, NSW. L. Copeland

Genus *Cadetia*

Diverse genus of c.60 spp., 5 in Aust., 2 endemic; others mainly in NG, few in Asia. Epiphytic orchids either forming small compact clumps of single-noded slender crowded stems or spreading patches with creeping rhizomes and short fleshy pseudobulbs. Leaf single on each stem or pseudobulb, with terminal papery bract enclosing floral meristems. Flowers white, produced singly or in small groups at sporadic intervals from within bract. NOTES: Ovaries and capsules smooth or burr-like from the presence of soft tubercles.

CLOSED BURR ORCHID *Cadetia clausa*

Jan–Jul. **ID: Small clumps; stems slender, flat, widening from base to apex; leaf dark green, thin-textured, notched; flowers not opening, borne singly, globose, white; ovary and capsule with fleshy tubercles.** Stems to 70 x 1.5mm. Leaves to 70 x 15mm. Flowers c.3mm across. **Dist.:** Qld (Moa Is.); 10–300m alt.; probably PNG. Rough-barked trees in rainforest. Flowers self-pollinate without opening. **Status:** Highly localised.

McILWRAITH BURR ORCHID *Cadetia collinsii*

Dec–Apr. **ID: Small clumps; stems slender, cylindrical, straight or curved; leaf on short stalk, dark green, fleshy, notched; flowers not opening widely, borne singly, white; sepals similar in shape and size; ovary and capsule with soft tubercles.** Stems to 18 x 2.5mm. Leaves to 30 x 10mm. Flowers 6–8mm across. **Dist.:** Qld (CYP – Iron Ra., Janet Ra., McIlwraith Ra.); 200–700m alt. Small rainforest trees along ridges, slopes and gorges on coastal side of ranges. Usually small groups. Flowers short-lasting (days). **Status:** Highly localised; vulnerable.

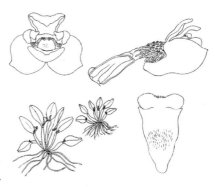

Cadetia collinsii

Cadetia clausa, Moa Is., Qld. M. Clements

C. clausa, Moa Is., Qld. M. Clements

C. collinsii, McIlwraith Ra., Qld. M. Clements

Cadetia collinsii, Rocky R., Qld. B. Lavarack

Cadetia collinsii, McIlwraith Ra., Qld. D. Titmuss

COASTAL BURR ORCHID *Cadetia maideniana*
Jan–Jul. **ID: Small clumps; stems slender, flat,
widening from base to apex; leaf dark green, thin-
textured, notched; flowers opening widely, borne
singly, cream/greenish to white; ovary and capsule
with fleshy hair-like tubercles.** Stems to 70 x 2mm.
Leaves to 60 x 15mm. Flowers 1–2, 5–6mm across.
Dist.: Qld (Bamaga to Townsville); 5–250m alt.
Coast and adjacent ranges on rocks and trees in
mangroves and rainforest, usually among moss in
shady situations. **Status:** Widespread, common.

Cadetia maideniana

SMOOTH BURR ORCHID *Cadetia taylorii*
Nov–May. **ID: Small crowded clumps; stems erect,
cylindrical, shallowly grooved; leaf dark green,
leathery, notched; flowers opening widely, white,
labellum white with yellow or pink; ovary and
capsule smooth.** Stems to 100 x 5mm. Leaves to
50 x 12mm. Flowers 1–2, 10–12mm across. **Dist.:**
Qld (Bamaga to Townsville); 5–1,600m alt.; also
PNG. Trees and rocks in rainforest, mangroves
and humid forests from sea level to mountain tops.
Status: Widespread, common.

Cadetia taylorii

CREEPING BURR ORCHID *Cadetia wariana*
Apr–Oct. **ID: Dense, branching, spreading mats;
pseudobulbs obliquely erect, ovoid, grey/green,
shiny, grooved; leaf on short stalk, dark green; fleshy;
flowers white, labellum and column with yellow/
orange tip; ovary and capsule smooth.** Pseudobulbs
to 10 x 3.5mm. Leaves to 15 x 5mm. Flowers 4–5mm
across. **Dist.:** Qld (Moa Is., CYP – McIlwraith Ra.,
Tozer Ra.); 50–400m alt.; also PNG. Rocks and
rough-barked trees close to watercourses; humid slopes
near rainforest. **Status:** Highly localised; vulnerable.

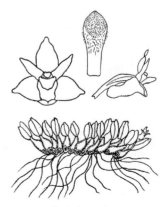

Cadetia wariana

Cadetia maideniana in fruit, Mossman Gorge, Qld. D. Banks

C. maideniana, Daintree R., Qld. D. Banks

Cadetia taylorii, Herberton Ra, Qld. D. Jones

C. taylorii, Mt Finnigan, Qld. D. Banks

Cadetia wariana, Iron Ra., Qld. M. Clements

C. wariana, Iron Ra., Qld. M. Clements

Genus *Davejonesia*

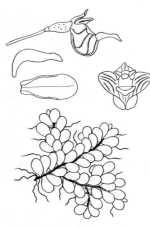

Davejonesia lichenastrum

Three spp. endemic in Aust. Small epiphytic orchids with thin creeping rhizomes (no pseudobulbs) clothed with papery bracts. Plants grow as extended strands or dense branching mats. Leaf single, thick, fleshy, attached alternately along the rhizomes. Small widely opening flowers arise singly on short thin stalks from the rhizome near the base of a recently mature leaf. Sepals much wider than petals.

ANGULAR BUTTON ORCHID *Davejonesia aurantiacopurpurea*

Nov-Feb, sporadic. **ID: Leaves prostrate to obliquely erect, ovoid to wedge-shaped, usually angular, dark green, bluntly pointed; flowers pink or mauve with orange/red stripes; labellum yellow/orange.** Leaves to 25 x 8mm. Flowers c.5 x 7mm. **Dist.:** Qld (Mt Lewis to Mt Spec); 100–1,200m alt. Trunks and larger branches of rainforest trees, rocks, boulders and cliff faces. **Status:** Locally common.

COMMON BUTTON ORCHID *Davejonesia lichenastra*

Sporadic. **ID: Leaves prostrate, button-like, elliptical to nearly circular, dark green; flowers white, cream or pink with red stripes; labellum orange.** Leaves to 10 x 7mm. Flowers c.5 x 7mm. **Dist.:** Qld (Mt Finnigan to Mackay); 400–1,400m alt. Dense patches on rainforest trees, rocks, boulders and cliff faces; humid slopes in open forest, especially above 500m altitude. Leaves reddish in sunny sites. **Status:** Widespread, common.

PILLAR ORCHID *Davejonesia prenticei*

Sporadic. **ID: Leaves erect, cylindrical/terete, thick, fleshy, straight or curved, dark green; flowers white, cream, pink or mauve with red stripes; labellum yellow/orange.** Leaves to 40 x 4mm. Flowers c.5 x 7mm. **Dist.:** Qld (Mt Finnigan to Mt Spec); 5–1,400m alt. Trunks and outer branches of rainforest trees; occas. on mangroves. Relict trees in paddocks. **Status:** Widespread, common.

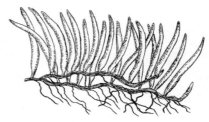

Davejonesia prenticei

Davejonesia aurantiacopurpurea, Millaa Millaa Qld

D. aurantiacopurpurea, Millaa Millaa, Qld. R. Tunstall

Davejonesia lichenastra, Tinaroo Dam, Qld. M. Clements

D. lichenastra, Mt Fox, Qld. M. Clements

Davejonesia prenticei, Deeral Landing, Qld. D. Banks

D. prenticei, Tinaroo Dam, Qld. D. Banks

Genus *Dichopus*

TARTAN ORCHID *Dichopus insignis*

Sporadic flowerer. **ID:** Single sp. extending to Aust. **Stems straggly, flattish, apical part often leafless; leaves in 2 alternate ranks, dark green; flowers in pairs, yellow with orange or red marks; labellum white with finger-like calli; sepals and petals triangular, curved.** Stems to 1m x 5mm. Leaves to 70 x 30mm. Flowers to 35 x 35mm. **Dist.:** Qld (Dauan Is., Saibai Is. in Torres Strait); 1–20m alt.; also PNG, Bougainville, Indon. Australian plants occur on mangroves. Stems continue growing for many years; apical leaves small compared with lower leaves. Flowers strongly fragrant, last 2–3 days. **Status:** Highly localised in Aust.

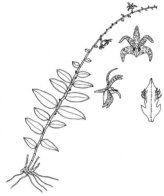

Dichopus insignis

Dichopus insignis, Sabai Is, Qld. D. Banks

Genus *Diplocaulobium*

Diplocaulobium glabrum

Diverse genus of c.105 spp. centred on Malaysia and Pacific, especially PNG, 1 sp. extending to Aust. Clumping epiphytic orchids with slender rhizomes, thin roots, 1-noded pseudobulbs swollen at base then narrowed with single, thin apical leaf. Flower single (often clustered in groups), arising sporadically from floral meristem within papery bract at top of pseudobulb. NOTES: Flowers on thin stalks, opening widely, short-lived (8–10 hours).

CREEPING STAR ORCHID *Diplocaulobium glabrum Sporadic flowerer.* **ID: Pseudobulbs yellow/green, shiny; leaf leathery, notched; flowers white with pale yellow tips; sepals and petals thin, tapered from base, spreading widely.** Pseudobulbs to 50 x 15mm. Leaves to 75 x 15mm. Flowers to 25 x 25mm. **Dist.:** Qld (Moa Is, Cape York to Whitfield Ra.); 5–500m alt.; also PNG. Conspicuous yellow/green clumps on trees in sparse rainforest; humid slopes and flats near streams in open forest. **Status:** Widespread, common.

Diplocaulobium glabrum, New Holland Reef Mine, Qld. D. Jones   *D. glabrum*, McIlwraith Ra., Qld. B. Lavarack

Genus *Dockrillia*

About 29 spp., 17 in Aust.; others in Timor, Indonesia, PNG, NCal., Vanuatu, Fiji, Samoa, Tahiti. Plants without pseudobulbs, either with creeping rhizomes and appressed leaves or with creeping rhizomes and branching aerial stems that form pendulous/hanging clumps (stems wiry, often yellow with age). Leaves thickened, fleshy, occas. button-like but more usually terete/cylindrical in shape, pendulous/arching away from the host. Flowers in short racemes arising from node near leaf base. NOTES: Plants creeping or hanging on trees and rocks. Flowers open widely.

BROWN ROCK ORCHID *Dockrillia banksii*
Sep–Nov. **ID: Clumps arching/pendulous, crowded, to 1m long; leaves terete, curved, green/reddish, shallowly grooved; flowers pink/brown with reddish internal stripes; labellum white with widely flared crinkled margins.** Stems to 1m x 2mm. Leaves to 180 x 2mm. Flowers 1–2, 25–35mm across. **Dist.:** NSW (Liverpool Ra. to Blue Mtns, Rylestone); 300–600m alt. Rocks, boulders and cliff faces in shrubby forest. Stems attached basally, upper parts hanging free with aerial roots. **Status:** Locally common. **See also:** *D. striolata.*

SMALL-FLOWERED PENCIL ORCHID *Dockrillia baseyana*
Aug–Nov. **ID: Clumps straggly; leaves terete, pendulous, dark green; racemes short; flowers well spaced, small, white/cream with short purple central stripes; labellum tapered to narrow point.** Leaves to 200 x 3mm. Flowers 2–5, 10–15mm across. **Dist.:** Qld (Mt Windsor Tlnd, Mt Finnigan, ?Kings Plains); 300–1,200m alt. Trees in rainforest. Poorly known sp. **Status:** Localised. **See also:** *D. calamiformis.*

Dockrillia brevicauda

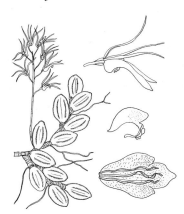

Dockrillia linguiformis

Dockrillia banksii, Awaba SF, NSW. L. Copeland

D. banksii, Awaba SF, NSW. L. Copeland

Dockrillia baseyana, Mt Lewis, Qld. D. Banks

D. baseyana, Mt Windsor Tlnd, Qld. D. Jones

STRAGGLY PENCIL ORCHID *Dockrillia bowmanii*

Aug–Nov; Feb–Jun. **ID:** Clumps semi-pendulous, straggly, sparsely branched; leaves terete, shallowly grooved; racemes short; flowers pale green to yellow/green or brownish; labellum white with crinkly margins. Stems to 600 x 4mm. Leaves to 150 x 4mm. Flowers 1–4, 20–25mm across. **Dist.:** Qld, NSW (Forty Mile Scrub to Woodburn); 5–800m alt.; also NCal. Trees and rocks in gorges, drier rainforest, vine forest, coastal scrub and littoral rainforest. All plants in area flower simultaneously in sporadic flushes. **Status:** Widespread, sporadic, locally common.

MT FINNIGAN PENCIL ORCHID *Dockrillia brevicauda*

Dec–Jan. **ID:** Clumps pendulous, slender, with long straight stems; leaves terete, ungrooved, thickish; racemes short, erect; flowers yellowish, brownish/yellow or orange/brown with red central stripes; labellum shortly pointed, margins wavy. Stems to 2m x 4mm. Leaves to 600 x 5mm. Flowers 5–8, 35–45mm across. **Dist.:** Qld (Mt Finnigan, Mt Misery); 700–950m alt. Trees, granite boulders and cliff faces in rainforest; tall trees in mist forest. Flowers fragrant. **Status:** Highly localised.

TABLELAND PENCIL ORCHID *Dockrillia calamiformis*

Aug–Nov. **ID:** Clumps pendulous, robust, untidy; leaves terete, ungrooved; racemes short; flowers white/cream with short red/purple central stripes; labellum with long, thin, whip-like point. Stems to 1m x 3mm. Leaves to 250 x 3mm. Flowers 3–5, 25–35mm across. **Dist.:** Qld (Mt Windsor Tlnd to Paluma Ra.); 500–1,200m alt. Trees, boulders and cliffs on ridges in rainforest; buoyant airy open forest where mists, clouds and drizzle are frequent. **Status:** Widespread, common. **See also:** *D. fasciculata.*

CUCUMBER ORCHID, GHERKIN ORCHID *Dockrillia cucumerina*

Sep–Mar. **ID:** Clumps appressed to host; stems creeping; leaves gherkin-like, widely spaced, dark green, covered with numerous bumps; racemes short; flowers cream, yellowish or greenish/white with purplish central stripes; labellum with 3 red wavy ridges and deeply folded/crinkled margins. Leaves to 35 x 12mm. Flowers 2–10, 12–20mm across. **Dist.:** Qld, NSW (Bunya Mtns to Picton); 50–1,000m alt. Uncommon/rare near coast, mainly ranges and well inland; rocks and large trees beside streams; often trunk and underside of larger branches of River Oak; Bunya Pines in drier forest. **Status:** Widespread, sporadic.

Dockrillia bowmanii, Bunya Mts, Qld. D. Banks

D. bowmanii, Woodburn, NSW. L. Copeland

Dockrillia brevicauda, Mt Finnigan, Qld. M. Harrison

D. brevicauda, Mt Finnigan, Qld. D. Banks

Dockrillia calamiformis, Mt Lewis, Qld. D. Banks

D. calamiformis, Millaa Millaa, Qld. M. Clements

D. cucumerina, Oxley Wild Rivers NP, NSW. L. Copeland

D. cucumerina flowers, Gara Gorge, NSW. L. Copeland

YELLOW PENCIL ORCHID *Dockrillia dolichophylla*

Jul–Sep. **ID: As for *Dockrillia fairfaxii* but with larger yellow flowers with purple/red central stripes; labellum with 3 strongly wavy ridges and long thin point.** Stems to 3m x 3mm. Leaves to 1m x 6mm. Flowers 1–6, 50–80mm across. **Dist.:** Qld, NSW (Eungella, Kroombit Tops to Dorrigo); 300–1,200m alt. Trees in wet rainforest, occas. rocks; Bunya Pines in drier rainforest; large river oaks beside streams; humid areas of open forest. **Status:** Widespread, locally common. **See also:** *D. fairfaxii.*

BLUE MOUNTAINS PENCIL ORCHID *Dockrillia fairfaxii*

Aug–Sep. **ID: Clumps pendulous with straight stems and aerial roots; leaves terete, dark green; racemes short; flowers white/cream with red central stripes; labellum with red stripes, wavy margins and long thin point.** Stems to 3m x 4mm. Leaves to 700 x 4mm. Flowers 1–4, 35–50mm across. **Dist.:** NSW (Gibralter Ra. to Blue Mtns); 300–1,000m alt. Mainly trees in rainforest, occas. rocks. **Status:** Localised, uncommon. **See also:** *D. dolichophylla.*

NORTHERN PENCIL ORCHID *Dockrillia fasciculata*

Aug–Nov. **ID: Clumps pendulous, robust, tiered with straight stems; leaves terete; racemes stiffly spreading; flowers crowded, white (often not opening widely), few short central purplish stripes; labellum with long fine point.** Stems to 2m x 4mm. Leaves to 400 x 8mm. Racemes 30–100mm. Flowers 6–12, 40–60mm across. **Dist.:** Qld (Cooktown to Townsville); 5–300m alt. Coast and adjacent ranges on trees and rocks in rainforest and humid open forest; occas. mangroves. Colonises trees in gardens, parks and paddocks. **Status:** Widespread, common. **See also:** *D. calamiformis.*

THUMBNAIL ORCHID, TICK ORCHID *Dockrillia linguiformis* var. *linguiformis*

Jun–Sep. **ID: Clumps appressed to host; stems creeping, much-branched; leaves tongue-shaped, appressed to stem, alternately arranged, thick, furrowed; racemes erect, conspicuous; flowers white with yellow labellum callus.** Leaves to 40 x 15mm. Racemes 60–150mm. Flowers 5–20, 8–13mm across. **Dist.:** Qld, NSW (Gympie to Mumbulla Mtn); 5–1,100m alt.; also NCal. Rocks, boulders, cliffs and trees in rainforest, gullies, gorges and forest, usually in bright light, often full sun. Flowers fragrant. **Status:** Widespread, common. **See also:** *D. nugentii.*

Dockrillia dolichophylla, Koreelah NP, NSW. L. Copeland

D. dolichophylla, Koreelah, NSW. L. Copeland

Dockrillia fairfaxii, Werrikimbe, NSW. L. Copeland

D. fairfaxii, Cottan-Bimbang NP, NSW. L. Copeland

Dockrillia fasciculata, Cape Tribulation, Qld. D. Jones

D. fasciculata, Cairns, Qld. D. Banks

Dockrillia linguiformis, The Gulf, NSW. D. Jones

D. linguiformis var. linguiformis, Alum Mtn, NSW. L. Copeland

NARROW THUMBNAIL ORCHID *Dockrillia linguiformis* var. *huntiana*

Jun–Sep. **ID: Differs from var. *linguiformis* by extremely narrow, drawn out leaves and smaller cream flowers that open widely. Dist.:** Qld, NSW (Mt Coot-Tha to Iluka). Trees in moist forests and along streambanks. Poorly known variant. **Status:** Highly localised.

SLENDER PENCIL ORCHID *Dockrillia mortii*

Sep–Nov. **ID: Clumps semi-pendulous, small, untidy, with dangling yellowish stems; leaves terete, green, grooved; racemes very short; flowers green to brownish; labellum white with purple marks and crinkled margins.** Stems to 700 x 1mm. Leaves to 100 x 4mm. Flowers 1–3, 17–20mm across. **Dist.:** Qld, NSW (Spicers Gap to Barrington Tops); 500–1,000m alt. Upper branches of rainforest trees, especially on high ridges with breezes, mists and fogs. Less common at lower alt. **Status:** Widespread, sporadic, locally common.

NORTHERN THUMBNAIL ORCHID *Dockrillia nugentii*

Jun–Sep. **ID: Similar to *D. linguiformis* but with oblong/round sandpaper-textured leaves and smaller cream flowers which don't open as widely and quickly age yellowish or brownish.** Leaves to 45 x 20mm. Racemes 60–150mm. Flowers 6–15, 6–9mm across. **Dist.:** Qld (Mt Finnigan to Eungella, Calliope Ra.); 600–1,000m alt. Trees and rocks in various moist to dry but humid habitats. Common on remnant trees in paddocks, parks and gardens. Flowers fragrant, often on one side of raceme. **Status:** Widespread, common.

DAGGER ORCHID *Dockrillia pugioniformis*

Sep–Nov. **ID: Clumps untidy, arching/ pendulous, with yellowish wiry stems and numerous aerial roots; leaves yellow/green, thick, fleshy, sometimes angular, tip rigid, sharply pointed; flower single, green to yellow/green; labellum white with purple lines and stains.** Stems to 2m x 4mm. Leaves to 70 x 20mm. Flowers 15–20mm across. **Dist.:** Qld, NSW (Bunya Mtns to Wyndham); 5–1,350m alt. Coast to mountains and well inland; trees and rocks in shady humid forest; moist ridges with buoyant air movement; less common in open or exposed habitats. **Status:** Widespread, common.

Dockrillia pugioniformis

D. linguiformis var. *huntiana*, Mororo Ck, NSW. L. Copeland

D. l. var. *h.*, Brunswick Heads, NSW. D. Banks

Dockrillia mortii, Washpool NP, NSW. L. Copeland

D. mortii flower, Washpool NP, NSW. L. Copeland

Dockrillia nugentii, Atherton, Qld. D. Jones

D. nugentii, Eungella, Qld. D. Banks

Dockrillia pugioniformis, Dorrigo, NSW. D. Banks

D. pugioniformis, Washpool, NSW. L. Copeland

UPRIGHT PENCIL ORCHID *Dockrillia racemosa*

Sep–Oct. **ID: Clumps sparse, upright, older stems arching/semi-pendulous; leaves terete, dark green, shallowly grooved; racemes erect; flowers cream to pale yellow; labellum with thread-like tip.** Stems to 1m x 6mm. Leaves to 200 x 12mm. Racemes 40–80mm long. Flowers 8–15, 20–25mm across. **Dist.:** Qld (Mt Windsor Tlnd to Paluma Ra.); 5–1500m alt.; 5–200m alt. Mainly trees in highland rainforest exposed to breezes, clouds and mists; much less common in lowland rainforest and mangroves. **Status:** Widespread, locally common.

SMOOTH TONGUE ORCHID *Dockrillia rigida*

Sporadic. **ID: Clumps small, pendulous, with short wiry stems attached by basal roots; leaves thick, smooth, dark green (often reddish tints); racemes short; flowers creamy/yellow; labellum with red/orange marks.** Stems to 400 x 3mm. Leaves to 60 x 15mm. Flowers 2–8, 12–15mm across. **Dist.:** Qld (Torres Strait Is., Cape York to Russell R.); 5–300m alt.; also PNG. Coast and adjacent ranges on rocks, rough-barked shrubs and trees; mangroves, coastal forest, rainforest margins, paperbark swamps, seasonally deciduous monsoon thickets. **Status:** Locally common.

COMMON PENCIL ORCHID *Dockrillia schoenina*

Jul–Nov. **ID: Clumps straggly, upright/sprawling, untidy, with wiry yellowish stems; leaves terete, green/yellowish, grooved, terete; flowers usually single, pale-coloured (white, greyish, green, pinkish or mauve) with mauve/purple stripes and marks.** Stems to 1m x 3mm. Leaves to 160 x 12mm. Flowers 1(–3), 25–35mm across. **Dist.:** Qld, NSW (Gladstone to Sydney); 100–750m alt. Rocks, cliff faces and trees in humid open forest, riverine forest and swampy habitats. Largest leaves occur near base of stems, small near tips. **Status:** Widespread, common.

STREAKED ROCK ORCHID *Dockrillia striolata* subsp. *striolata*

Sep–Nov. **ID: Clumps dense, spreading, with arching/pendulous yellowish stems attached by basal roots; leaves terete, erect/pendulous, curved, green/reddish; flowers greenish, cream or yellow with red/brown stripes; labellum white.** Stems to 600 x 2mm. Leaves to 120 x 4mm. Flowers 1–2, 15–20mm across. **Dist.:** NSW (N to Wingen), Vic (E), Tas (Flinders Is., Cape Barren Is.); 0–800m alt. Coast to mountains on rocks, boulders and cliff faces in shrubby forest; rarely on base of trees. Dense clumps, occas. extensive masses. **Status:** Widespread, common.

Dockrillia racemosa, Mt Windsor Tlnd, Qld. D. Banks

D. racemosa, Ravenshoe, Qld. D. Banks

Dockrillia rigida, Archer Point, Qld. J. Roberts

D. rigida, Cape York, Qld. D. Banks

Dockrillia schoenina, Wauchope, NSW. L. Copeland

D. schoenina, Barrington Tops, NSW. D. Banks

D. striolata subsp. *striolata*, Mt York, NSW. M. Harrison

D. s. subsp. *striolata*, near Nowra, NSW. A. Stephenson

GOLDEN ROCK ORCHID *Dockrillia striolata* subsp. *chrysantha*

Sep–Oct. **ID: Differs from subsp. *striolata* by its slightly larger flowers with bright butter yellow sepals that lack stripes or are very faintly striped and flared labellum with more strongly crinkled margins. Dist.:** Tas (E coast, St Marys to Coles Bay); 0–50m alt. Large coastal granite boulders in open forest where sea mists and fogs are frequent. **Status:** Locally common.

CAPE YORK PENCIL ORCHID *Dockrillia sulphurea*

Aug–Nov. **ID: Clumps pendulous, tiered; leaves terete, green, pendulous, ungrooved; racemes spreading; flowers pale sulphur-yellow with numerous reddish central spots and short streaks.** Stems to 1.5m x 4mm. Leaves to 350 x 6mm. Racemes 35–65mm. Flowers 5–10, 35–45mm across. **Dist.:** Qld (CYP – Cape York to Pascoe R.); 5–250m alt. Trees, rocks and boulders in rainforest, rockpile vegetation, sheltered gullies and humid areas of open forest. Flowers strongly scented. **Status:** Locally common.

BRIDAL VEIL ORCHID *Dockrillia teretifolia*

Jul–Oct. **ID: Clumps pendulous, slender to bushy; stems pendulous with protruding nodal spurs; leaves terete, pendulous, dark green, ungrooved; racemes spreading; flowers scented, white, cream or greenish with short red/purple central stripes.** Stems to 2m x 4mm. Leaves to 600 x 6mm. Racemes 50–100mm. Flowers 3–15, 30–40mm across. **Dist.:** Qld, NSW (Calliope Ra. to Narooma); 5–800m alt. Coast to ranges in wetter forests; trees and rocks near streams, lakes and coastal swamps; also mangroves. Often on Hoop Pine, figs and Swamp Oak. **Status:** Widespread, common.

RIBBED PENCIL ORCHID *Dockrillia wassellii*

May–Jun. **ID: Clumps appressed to host; stems creeping, thick, branched; leaves stiffly upright, elliptic-terete, green, hard, deeply furrowed; racemes erect; flowers crystalline white, crowded; labellum yellow with purple-spots.** Leaves to 120 x 10mm. Racemes 100–200mm. Flowers 10–60, 15–20mm across. **Dist.:** Qld (CYP – Iron Ra., McIlwraith Ra.); 100–400m alt. Upper branches of tall emergent trees, particularly hoop pine, in monsoonal rainforest, along stream banks and humid slopes; occas. on boulders. **Status:** Highly localised; vulnerable.

Dockrillia wassellii

Dockrillia striolata subsp. *chrysantha*, Bicheno, Tas. I. Johnson

Dockrillia sulphurea, Iron Ra., Qld. D. Banks

D. sulphurea, New Holland Reef Mine, Qld. D. Jones

Dockrillia teretifolia, Mangrove Ck, NSW. D. Banks

D. teretifolia, Mangrove Ck, NSW. D. Banks

Dockrillia wassellii, McIlwraith Ra., Qld. D. Banks

D. wassellii, McIlwraith Ra., Qld. D. Banks

NAMED NATURAL HYBRIDS

MANGROVE PENCIL ORCHID *Dockrillia ×foederata*
Oct–Jan. **ID:** Rare natural hybrid intermediate between *D. rigida* and *D. fasciculata* with sparsely branched pendulous stems, terete or flattish leaves to 120 x 5mm and 3–8-flowered racemes with white or cream flowers c.20mm across with purplish markings on labellum. **Dist.:** Qld (near mouth of Barron R.). **Notes:** Original plant was collected from a mangrove swamp that has now been cleared.

Dockrillia ×foederata, Barron R., Qld. D. Banks   *D. ×grimesii*, Atherton Tlnd, Qld. M. Harrison

HYBRID PENCIL ORCHID *Dockrillia ×grimesii*
Apr–Aug. **ID:** Rare natural hybrid between *D. calamiformis* and *D. nugentii* with creeping sparsely branched stems, terete or flattish grooved leaves to 150 x 9mm and 6–12-flowered racemes with white, cream or pinkish flowers c.25mm across with few purple markings. **Dist.:** Qld (Annan R. to Burdekin R., Atherton Tlnd, Evelyn Tlnd, Mt Spurgeon, Mt Stuart, ?Mt Spec). **Notes:** Grows with parents on exposed rainforest trees above 1,000m altitude.

Genus *Durabaculum*

About 76 spp., 13 spp. in N Aust., 7 endemic; also Pacific.
Variable genus best treated in groups. All plants have hard
pseudobulbs but grouping depends on pseudobulb features
(size, shape) and leaf details (arrangement, longevity and shape).

DURABACULUM IS DIVIDED INTO 5 GROUPS

GROUP 1: PSEUDOBULBS ELONGATED; LEAVES SCATTERED ALONG PSEUDOBULBS, LONG-LIVED, FLAT/CONCAVE; PETALS USUALLY TWISTED.

Durabaculum dalbertisii

GREEN ANTELOPE ORCHID *Durabaculum dalbertisii*

Mar–Dec. **ID: Pseudobulbs stiffly erect, cylindrical; leaves rigid, dark green; racemes
erect; flowers white with stiffly erect pale green petals that are twisted; labellum white
with purple veins.** Pseudobulbs to 600 x 25mm. Leaves to 140 x 40mm. Racemes to
350mm. Flowers to 60 x 50mm. **Dist.:** Qld (Sabai Is., CYP – E gorges of McIlwraith Ra.);
2–550m alt.; also PNG. Upper branches of rainforest trees and wattles in open humid
situations along stream banks and gorges. Flowers long-lived, fragrant. **Status:** Highly
localised; endangered.

Durabaculum dalbertisii, McIlwraith Ra., Qld. M. Clements   *D. dalbertisii*, McIlwraith Ra., Qld. D. Banks

DARK-STEMMED ANTLER ORCHID *Durabaculum mirbelianum*

Aug–Nov. **ID: Pseudobulbs cylindrical, dark black/brown; leaves often suffused with brown or dark red/purple; flowers brown; tepals not twisted; labellum yellow with dark red veins.** Pseudobulbs to 1m x 30mm. Leaves to 150 x 40mm. Racemes to 300mm. Flowers 30–40mm across. **Dist.:** Qld (Dauan Is., Daintree to Innisfail); 2–150m alt.; also Pacific Is. Trees and rocks in mangroves and humid coastal swamps in sunny situations. Some plants have wide-opening flowers, others remain semi-closed. **Status:** Uncommon, sporadic; endangered.

BLUE ANTELOPE ORCHID *Durabaculum nindii*

Jul–Sep. **ID: Pseudobulbs stiffly erect, cylindrical, dark brown/blackish; leaves large, dark green, concave; flowers flamboyant, mauve and white; petals twisted; labellum white with mauve/purple veins.** Pseudobulbs to 2.5m x 40mm. Leaves to 160 x 50mm. Racemes to 500mm. Flowers 50–60mm across. **Dist.:** Qld (Iron Ra., McIlwraith Ra. to Innisfail); 5–400m alt.; also PNG, Indon. Trees and palm trunks in hot humid near-coastal swamps, coastal rainforest and mangroves; stream banks and gorges in McIlwraith Ra. **Status:** Highly localised; endangered.

GOLDEN ORCHID *Durabaculum brownii* subsp. *brownii* ms.

Aug–Nov. **ID: Large untidy clumps; pseudobulbs cane-like, green to blackish; leaves green to yellowish, concave; flowers brown to yellow/ brown; tepals twisted/wavy; labellum with outcurved lateral lobes and mauve/purple marks.** Pseudobulbs to 5m x 60mm. Leaves to 160 x 50mm. Racemes to 600mm. Flowers 40–80mm across. **Dist.:** Qld (Cape York to 1770, many offshore islands); 0–800m alt. Coast (coral, beach sand, rocks and trees in coastal scrub, mangroves, rainforest) to ranges (trees and cliff faces in sparse rainforest, open forest, scrubby thickets and paddock trees), usually in exposed sunny situations. Abundant aerial growths. Previously well known as *Dendrobium undulatum* and *D. discolor*. **Status:** Widespread, common.

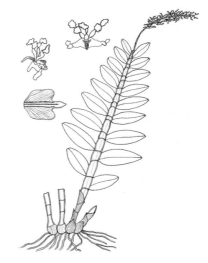

Durabaculum brownii subsp. *brownii*.

D. mirbellianum, Daintree R., Qld. J. Roberts

D. mirbelianum, Russell R., Qld. R. Tunstall

Durabaculum nindii growing on mangroves, Daintree R., Qld. J. Roberts

D. nindii, Daintree R., Qld. J. Roberts

D. brownii subsp. *brownii*, Hinchinbrook Is., Qld. J. Mohondas

D. b. subsp. *brownii*, Massey Creek, Qld. D. Banks

CANARY ORCHID *Durabaculum brownii* subsp. *brownii* 'Broomfield's variant'
Apr–Dec. **ID: Differs from subsp.** *undulatum* **by its green/yellow, golden/yellow or canary-yellow flowers with varnished lustre and labellum with outcurved lateral lobes and prominent white callus. Dist.:** Qld (Whitsunday Is. Group), 0–10m alt. Coastal scrub, headlands and rocks in full sun. Reproduces vegetatively by aerial growths. **Status:** Locally common.

BROWN ANTLER ORCHID *Durabaculum brownii* subsp. *discolor* ms.
Apr–Dec. **ID: Differs from subsp.** *undulatum* **by its shorter racemes (to 400mm long), with smaller red/brown to dark brown flowers (30–50mm across), labellum with strongly incurved lateral lobes (almost forming a tunnel) and mauve/purple marks. Dist.:** Qld (Torres Strait Is., Cape York to Mackay); 5–250m alt.; also PNG. Coastal scrub, littoral rainforest and mangroves. Numerous aerial growths. **Status:** Locally common.

GROUP 2: PSEUDOBULBS ELONGATED; LEAVES MAINLY ON UPPER NODES, LONG-LIVED (DECIDUOUS IN DROUGHT), NARROW, FLATTISH; SEPALS and PETALS TWISTED.

CHOCOLATE TEATREE ORCHID *Durabaculum johannis*
Mar–Jul. **ID: Pseudobulbs dark brown or purplish/brown; leaves dark green to purplish/green, sheath often with purple stripes; flowers smelly, chocolate-brown with bright yellow labellum.** Pseudobulbs to 300 x 15mm. Leaves to 200 x 15mm. Racemes to 250mm. Flowers 2–20, 20–40mm across. **Dist.:** Qld (Torres Strait Is., CYP – Cape York to McIlwraith Ra.); 50–600m alt. Trees in open humid woodland, swamps and monsoon thickets. Plants deciduous in long dry spells. Unpleasant floral scent. **Status:** Locally common; vulnerable.

YELLOW TEATREE ORCHID *Durabaculum trilamellatum*
Jul–Nov. **ID: Pseudobulbs green; leaves green; flowers yellow, yellow/brown, brown or grey/brown with darker stripes and tips; labellum mauve to purple with yellow midlobe.** Pseudobulbs to 600 x 25mm. Leaves to 250 x 15mm. Racemes to 500mm. Flowers 6–15, 40–60mm across. **Dist.:** NT (Cobourg Pen., Tiwi Is.), Qld (Cape York to Cooktown); 50–300m alt; also PNG. Rough-barked trees and paperbarks in humid forest, swamps and near streams, often close to coast. Sweet floral scent. **Status:** Locally common.

D. brownii subsp. *brownii* 'Broomfield's variant', Gloucester Is., Qld. R. Tunstall

Durabaculum brownii subsp. *discolor* ms, Qld. R. Tunstall

Durabaculum johannis, Punsan Bay, Qld. R. Tunstall

D. johannis, McIlwraith Ra., Qld. D. Jones

Durabaculum trilamellatum, near Cooktown, Qld. J. Roberts

D. trilamellatum, Melville Is., NT. R. Tunstall

GROUP 3: PSEUDOBULBS SHORT, SWOLLEN, ONION-SHAPED; LEAVES 2–6, TERMINAL ON PSEUDOBULBS, LONG-LIVED, NEARLY CYLINDRICAL, DEEPLY CHANNELLED; PETALS USUALLY TWISTED.

BROWN TEATREE ORCHID *Durabaculum canaliculatum*
Aug–Nov. **ID:** Flowers opening widely, light brown with darker tips; sepals and petals twisted near apex; labellum white with purple streaks. Pseudobulbs to 120 x 30mm. Leaves to 250 x 12mm. Racemes to 400mm. Flowers 5–30, 25–30mm across. **Dist.:** Qld (Torres Strait Is., Cape York to near Laura and Cooktown); 5–700m alt.; also PNG. Exposed sites on trees in humid sparse woodland, grassy forest, swamps and stream banks. **Status:** Locally common.

Durabaculum canaliculatum

PINK TEATREE ORCHID *Durabaculum carronii*
Aug–Oct. **ID:** Pseudobulbs green or purplish; leaves 2–4, green to purplish; flowers opening widely; sepals white, c.3mm long; petals c. 20mm long, pink with dark brown and purple marks, twisted once; labellum yellow. Pseudobulbs to 50 x 30mm. Leaves to 120 x 5mm. Racemes to 200mm. Flowers 2–12, 18–25mm across. **Dist.:** Qld (Torres Strait Is., CYP – Cape York to McIlwraith Ra.); 5–700m alt.; also PNG. Stunted trees, often paperbarks, in sparse woodland on slopes and swamps. Often in full sun. **Status:** Locally common; vulnerable.

Durabaculum canaliculatum, Coen, Qld. D. Jones

D. canaliculatum, Cooktown, Qld. D. Banks

Durabaculum carronii, McIlwraith Ra., Qld. D. Jones

D. carronii, McIlwraith Ra., Qld. D. Jones

THIN TEATREE ORCHID *Durabaculum foelschei*

Jul–Sep. **ID: Pseudobulbs often drawn-out; flowers often cupped, white with yellow or tan tips; labellum white with purple streaks.** Pseudobulbs to 120 x 20mm. Leaves to 180 x 8mm. Racemes to 250mm. Flowers 5–40, 22–36mm across. **Dist.:** WA (Kimberley Region), NT (N), Qld (Torres Strait Is., CYP – Cape York to Wenlock R.); 0–200m alt.; also PNG. Trees (often paperbarks) close to swamps, billabongs and streams; stunted coastal forest and scrub. **Status:** Widespread, common.

SOUTHERN TEATREE ORCHID *Durabaculum tattonianum*

Jul–Sep. **ID: Flowers opening widely, white with yellow or light brown tips; labellum white with purple streaks and marks.** Pseudobulbs to 120 x 25mm. Leaves to 200 x 8mm. Racemes to 300mm. Flowers 5–50, 22–30mm across. **Dist.:** Qld (Laura to Rockhampton); 5–1,000m alt. Mainly coastal but also ranges and tlnds; trees in stunted forest, mangroves, swamps and woodland dominated by Broad-leaved Paperbark. **Status:** Widespread, common.

GROUP 4: PSEUDOBULBS ELONGATED, LEAFY IN UPPER THIRD; LEAVES FLAT, SHEDDING AFTER C.12 MONTHS; FLORAL SEGMENTS NOT TWISTED; PETALS MUCH WIDER THAN SEPALS.

MAUVE BUTTERFLY ORCHID

Durabaculum bigibbum

Feb–Jul. **ID: Pseudobulbs tall, green or purplish; leaves often with purplish margins; flowers large, showy, lilac/purple; petals broad; labellum with prominent white spot.** Pseudobulbs to 1.2m x 15mm. Leaves to 150 x 35mm. Racemes to 400mm. Flowers 2–20, 30–60mm wide. Petals 25–30mm across. **Dist.:** Qld (Torres Strait is., CYP – Cape York to Archer R., Mapoon, Weipa); 0–400m alt. Among rubble and litter on coastal cliffs; trees and rocks in stunted coastal scrub, streambank vegetation, monsoon thickets; open areas and gullies in sparse forest. **Status:** Locally common; vulnerable.

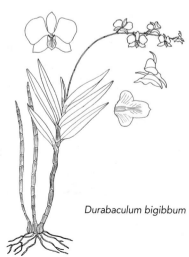

Durabaculum bigibbum

Durabaculum foelschei, Berry Springs, NT. M. Clements

D. foelschei, Cooinda, NT. M. Clements

Durabaculum tattonianum, Mt Garnet, Qld. D. Banks

D. tattonianum, Mt Garnet, Qld. D. Banks

Durabaculum bigibbum, Tozer Ra., Qld. D. Banks

D. bigibbum, Bamaga, Qld. M. Clements

WHITE BUTTERFLY ORCHID *Durabaculum dicuphum*

(Mar–) May–Aug. **ID: Pseudobulbs covered with white sheath; flowers white; petals broad; labellum white with yellow or purple basal blotch.** Pseudobulbs to 700 x 25mm. Leaves to 200 x 30mm. Racemes to 500mm. Flowers 2–20, 25–50mm across. Petals 8–10mm wide. **Dist.:** WA (Kimberley Region), NT (N, Tiwi Is., Groote Eylandt); 0–300m alt. Trees in monsoon thickets, littoral rainforest, streamside vegetation, lagoons, swamps, woodland, landward side of mangroves. Flowers short lasting and may not open fully. **Status:** Widespread, locally common.

COOKTOWN ORCHID *Durabaculum phalaenopsis*

Mar–Jul. **ID: Similar to *D. bigibbum* but with short to tall, conical to cylindrical pseudobulbs and lilac-purple flowers; labellum darker purple labellum, no white spot.** Pseudobulbs 0.2–1.2m x 15mm. Leaves to 150 x 35mm. Racemes to 400mm. Flowers 2–20, 50–80mm across. Petals 25–30mm wide. **Dist.:** Qld (Cooktown to Font Hills, Daintree to Cairns); 5–800m alt. Trees and rocks in coastal scrub, littoral rainforest, riverine vegetation, monsoon thickets, vine thickets, swamps and gullies in open forest. A compact growing variant with short pseudobulbs occurs in S parts of its range. **Status:** Locally common; vulnerable.

Durabaculum phalaenopsis, Font Hills, Qld. J. Roberts

Durabaculum dicuphum, Mt Borradaile, NT.
M. Clements

D. dicuphum, Berry Springs, NT. M. Clements

Durabaculum phalaenopsis, Font Hills, Qld. J. Roberts

GROUP 5: PSEUDOBULBS SHORT, SWOLLEN; LEAVES FLAT, SHEDDING AFTER C.12 MONTHS; FLORAL SEGMENTS NOT TWISTED; SEPALS MUCH WIDER THAN PETALS.

DAMSEL ORCHID *Durabaculum fellowsii*

Oct–Jan. **ID: Small clumping plants; pseudobulbs short, dark brown; leaves short-lived, dark green; flowers pale green or yellowish; labellum purple, midlobe deeply notched.** Pseudobulbs to 250 x 10mm. Leaves to 100 x 20mm. Racemes to 80mm. Flowers 2–7, 20–25mm across. **Dist.:** Qld (Mt Windsor Tlnd, Mt Finnigan to Paluma); 700–1,200m alt. Shrubs and trees with rough stringy or flaky bark in humid forest; rocky slopes close to gullies with ephemeral streams. Also called *Eleutheroglossum fellowsii*. **Status:** Sporadic, localised; vulnerable.

Durabaculum fellowsii

NAMED NATURAL HYBRID

CURLY PINKS *Durabaculum ×superbiens*

Dec–Jun. **ID:** Natural hybrid between *D. bigibbum* and *D. brownii* subsp. *brownii* with long cylindrical pseudobulbs, tough dark green leaves and long racemes of showy pink to reddish/mauve flowers 35–45mm across, the sepals and petals twisted and wavy. **Dist.:** Qld (Thursday Is., Cape York to Portland Roads); 0–150m alt. **Notes:** Low trees or rocks in stunted coastal scrub. Flowers colourful and long-lasting. Variable hybrid that can backcross to parents.

Durabaculum ×superbiens

Durabaculum fellowsii, Herberton Ra., Qld. D. Banks

D. fellowsii, Herberton Ra., Qld. M. Clements

Durabaculum ×superbiens, Cape York, Qld. E. Rotherham

Genus *Flickingeria*

About 70 spp., 2 endemic in Aust., *F. nativitatas* on Christmas Is. (page 000); others in tropical Asia, Pacific Is. Plants either have creeping branched stems appressed to the host (*F. convexa*) or aerial stems that branch irregularly from upper nodes (*F. clementsii*, *F. nativitis*). Leaf single per pseudobulb. Flowers short-lived (hours) produced singly or in small groups at sporadic intervals in the flowering period.

CRIMP ORCHID *Flickingeria clementsii*
Sporadic. **ID: Straggly clumps with arching/semi-pendulous aerial stems** and **deeply grooved pseudobulbs; leaves dark green, progressively smaller along each stem; flowers in clusters, cream with purple-spots; labellum apex densely fringed.** Stems to 1m. Pseudobulbs to 300 x 5mm. Leaves to 220 x 100mm. Flowers 20–25mm across. **Dist.:** Qld (CYP–Iron Ra., McIlwraith Ra.); 100–500m alt. Trees and rocks in rainforest. All plants in area flower synchronously. **Status:** Highly localised.

PIGGYBACK ORCHID *Flickingeria convexa*
Sporadic. **ID: Creeping sp. appressed to host with widely spaced, stalked, shiny green pseudobulbs; leaves petiolate, dark green; flower single, cream, arising from leaf base; labellum red and yellow, apex with 2 oblong lobes.** Pseudobulbs to 50 x 10mm. Leaves to 80 x 15mm. Racemes to 80mm. Flowers 12–15mm across. **Dist.:** Qld (Iron Ra. to Daintree R.); 0–700m alt.; also Asia, Pacific Is. Mangroves, coastal forest, rainforest and humid areas of open forest and heath. **Status:** Highly localised.

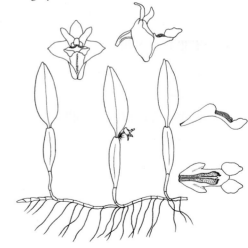

Flickingeria clementsii   *Flickingeria convexa*

Flickingeria clementsii, Leo Creek, Qld. M. Harrison

F. clementsii, Iron Ra., Qld. M. Clements

Flickingeria convexa, McIlwraith Ra., Qld. M. Clements

F. convexa, McIlwraith Ra., Qld. M. Clements

Genus *Grastidium*

About 200 spp., 5 in Aust., 3 endemic; others in Pacific Is. Clumping epiphytic or lithophytic orchids with thin leafy flattened stems (no pseudobulbs) that continue growth over 2–3 seasons. Flowers, produced in sporadic bursts throughout year, arise on stem opposite a leaf, singly or in pairs, lasting few hours or 1–2 days; paired flowers face inwards towards each other. NOTES: In some sp. the floral segments tangle as flowers age.

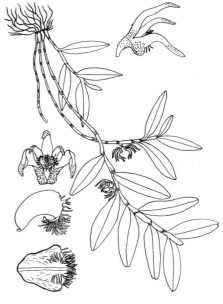

Grastidium cancroides

BLOTCHED GEMINI ORCHID
Grastidium baileyi

Jan–Feb, sporadic. **ID: Stems arching/willowy, thin; leaves crowded, dark green; flowers paired, yellow/green, spidery, densely spotted and blotched with red/purple; segments narrow, long-pointed, spreading widely for few hours.** Stems to 1.2m x 3mm. Leaves to 90 x 8mm. Flowers 20–30mm across. **Dist.:** Qld (McIlwraith Ra. to Paluma Ra., Bowen); 5–900m alt.; also NG, Solomon Is. Mainly coastal, less common in ranges; trees in lowland rainforest, swamps, monsoon thickets and mangroves lining large streams and estuaries. **Status:** Widespread, locally common.

CRAB ORCHID *Grastidium cancroides*

Dec–May. **ID: Stems suberect to pendulous, brownish, roughened, widening towards apex; leaves on upper half of stem, dark green, shiny, base warty; flowers paired, warty, red/brown with yellow central area; segments incurved, petals often twisted.** Stems to 800 x 6mm. Leaves to 100 x 35mm. Flowers 18–22mm across. **Dist.:** Qld (McIlwraith Ra. to Johnstone R.); 0–600m alt. Trees in moist, shady, humid rainforest, especially overhanging watercourses. **Status:** Highly localised.

Grastidium baileyi, Millaa Millaa, Qld. D. Jones

G. baileyi, Palmerston NP, Qld. M. Clements

Grastidium cancroides, Mossman Gorge, Qld. B. Lavarack

G. cancroides, Mossman Gorge, Qld. M. Harrison

HONEY ORCHID *Grastidium luteocilium*

Jan–Mar, sporadic. **ID: Stems erect, arching or pendulous, thick, yellowish; leaves large, thick, leathery, yellow/green; flowers paired, dull yellow or greenish, honey-scented; labellum with central patch of yellow hairs.** Stems to 2m x 15mm. Leaves to 120 x 45mm. Flowers 17–20mm across. **Dist.:** Qld (Moa Is., Iron Ra. to near Tully); 0–350m alt.; also NG. Coastal lowlands and adjacent ranges on trees and rocks in rainforest. Often strongly bleached by sun. **Status:** Widespread, common.

HERMIT ORCHID *Grastidium malbrownii*

Dec–Apr. **ID: Stems crowded, suberect to arching, very thin; leaves narrow, dark green, shiny, deeply notched; flower single, cream, shiny; labellum purple and yellow, constricted near apex.** Stems to 300 x 1mm. Leaves to 60 x 4mm. Flowers 7–8mm across. **Dist.:** Qld (CYP – McIlwraith Ra.); 300–600m alt., Trees, palms, logs and rocks in moist humid rainforest. **Status:** Highly localised, locally common.

WHITE GEMINI ORCHID *Grastidium tozerense*

Jan–Mar, sporadic. **ID: Stems erect to willowy, thin, wiry; leaves narrow, dark green; flowers paired, white; labellum white, sparsely hairy.** Stems to 600 x 2mm. Leaves to 80 x 8mm. Flowers 30–35mm across. **Dist.:** Qld (CYP – McIlwraith Ra., Tozer Ra., Iron Ra.); 300–550m alt. Rocks and large boulders in rockpile vegetation; trees and cliff faces near waterfalls; occas. upper branches of trees in rainforest. Usually in bright light. **Status:** Highly localised; vulnerable.

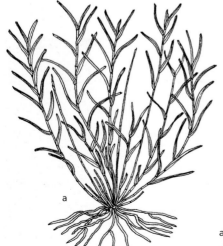

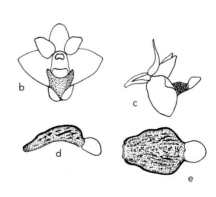

Grastidium malbrownii

a) plant; b) flower from front; c) flower from side;
d) lanbellum from side; e) labellum flattened

Grastidium luteocilium, Iron Ra., Qld. D. Banks

G. luteocilium, Daintree, Qld. D. Banks

Grastidium malbrownii, Leo Creek, Qld. D. Banks

G. malbrownii, Leo Ck, Qld. E. Rotherham

Grastidium tozerense, Iron Ra., Qld. M. Clements

G. tozerense, Iron Ra., Qld. M. Clements

Genus *Sayeria*

About 77 spp., 1 extending to Aust.; others in Indon., NG. Clumping epiphytic orchids with hard, swollen pseudobulbs that are often basally stalked, leaves apical on pseudobulbs and racemes arising from upper nodes with the colourful stalked flowers grouped at apex of long peduncle. NOTES: Flowers long lasting.

Sayeria bifalcis

NATIVE BEE ORCHID *Sayeria bifalcis*

Apr–Jul. **ID: Pseudobulbs yellowish or purplish; leaves 2–4, dark green to yellowish, leathery; racemes stiffly erect; flowers in apical group, greenish/yellow with purple-brown stripes and spots.** Pseudobulbs to 400 x 25mm. Leaves to 150 x 50mm. Racemes to 250mm. Flowers 5–10, 25–35mm across. **Dist.:** Qld (Moa Is., Dauan Is., CYP – Cape York to McIlwraith Ra., ?Daintree R.); 0–500m alt.; also NG. Trees and boulders lining streams in humid rainforest in brightly lit situations. Often bleached by sun. **Status:** Locally common.

Sayeria bifalcis, Tozer's Gap Qld, M. Harrison

S. bifalcis, Iron Range, Qld. D. Banks

Genus *Stilbophyllum*

SPARKLE ORCHID, MICA ORCHID *Stilbophyllum toressae*

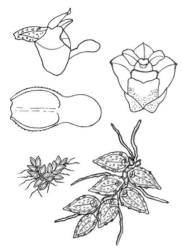

Sporadic. **ID:** Single sp. endemic in Aust. **Small creeping epiphyte/lithophyte forming dense mats; pseudobulbs absent; leaves deeply concave, dark green to reddish, sparkling/glittering, basal sunken area with papery bract; flowers arise singly from basal bract, stalkless, cream with yellow labellum.** Leaves to 8 x 4mm. Racemes to 80mm. Flowers c.6mm across. **Dist.:** Qld (Big Tlnd to Tully Falls); 10–1,600m alt. Coast to high alt. on tlnds; trees and rocks in rainforest and other moist humid forest. **Status:** Locally common.

Stilbophyllum toressae

Stilbophilum toressae, Tinaroo Hills, Qld. M. Harrison

S. toressae, Beatrice R., Qld. D. Banks

Genus *Thelychiton*

About 20 spp., mainly Aust.; *T. howeanus* and *T. moorei* on Lord Howe Is. (page 204), *T. brachypus*, *T. macropus* on Norfolk Is. (page 210); others in NCal., Vanuatu, Fiji. Clumping epiphytic/lithophytic orchids with hard, cylindrical, tapered, or tetragonal pseudobulbs, leaves apical on pseudobulbs and relatively large flowers, often colourful, on multiflowered racemes from upper axillary nodes.

Thelychiton kingianus

THELYCHITON IS DIVIDED INTO 2 MAIN GROUPS

GROUP 1: ROCK OR TREE-DWELLING ORCHIDS WITH TOUGH FIBROUS PSEUDOBULBS, MOSTLY CYLINDRICAL OR FUSIFORM (SPINDLE-SHAPED).

SLENDER CANE ORCHID *Thelychiton adae*
Jul–Oct. **ID: Pseudobulbs thin, yellowish; leaves dark green; racemes short; flowers usually white, occas. greenish, yellow or apricot-coloured; petals often paler than sepals; labellum white or green with short hairs.** Pseudobulbs to 600 x 6mm. Leaves 2–4, to 80 x 25mm. Racemes to 40mm. Flowers 1–5(–8), 20–30mm across. **Dist.:** Qld (Big Tlnd to Mt Spec); 700–1,300m alt. Rocks and trees in montane/highland rainforest/mist forest; sheltered slopes and ridges in humid open forest. Sweet floral scent. **Status:** Widespread, common.

GORGE ROCK ORCHID *Thelychiton carnarvonensis*
Aug–Nov. **ID: Similar to *T. kingianus* but with smaller pseudobulbs, longer narrower dark green to bluish leaves and pale pink flowers; labellum with purple stripes and green central line, but no ridges.** Pseudobulbs to 150 x 15mm. Leaves 2–7, to 140 x 20mm. Racemes to 150mm. Flowers 20–22mm across. **Dist.:** Qld (Carnarvon Gorge to Isla Gorge); 500–800m alt. Inland gorges and rocky sites beside streams. Extensive dense masses of intertwined stems. **Status:** Localised, locally common.

Thelychiton adae, Mt Lewis, Qld. D. Banks

T. adae, Mt Baldy, Qld. M. Harrison

Thelychiton carnarvonensis, Carnarvon Gorge, Qld.
R. Tunstall

T. carnarvonensis, Expedition Ra., Qld. M. Clements

BEECH ORCHID *Thelychiton falcorostrus*

Aug–Oct. **ID: Pseudobulbs crowded, spindle-shaped, yellow/green; leaves dark green, leathery; flowers crowded, crystalline white, strongly fragrant; labellum ending in upcurved beak-like point.** Pseudobulbs to 500 x 15mm. Leaves 2–5, to 150 x 30mm. Racemes to 160mm. Flowers 5–20, 30–35mm across. **Dist.:** Qld, NSW (Lamington Plateau to Barrington Tops.); (300–) 800–1,500m alt. Cool temperate rainforest; mainly upper trunks and larger branches of Antarctic Beech; less commonly boulders and other rainforest trees. Clouds and mists frequent. **Status:** Sporadic, locally common.

MT FINNIGAN CANE ORCHID *Thelychiton finniganensis*

Nov–Jan. **ID: Pseudobulbs thin, pale green/yellowish, numerous aerial growths; leaves dark green, thin-textured; flowers cream/white with yellow and purple central suffusions; labellum white with purple/red marks.** Pseudobulbs to 240 x 4mm. Leaves 1–3, to 80 x 20mm. Racemes to 45mm. Flowers 1–2(–5), 25–35mm across. **Dist.:** Qld (summits of Mt Finnigan, Mt Pieter Botte, Thornton Peak); 1,000–1,350m alt. Exposed sites among rocks, boulders, scattered low shrubs and dense *Lomandra* tussocks on mountain tops. Frequents mists and fogs. Dense vegetative colonies. **Status:** Highly localised, locally common.

APRICOT CANE ORCHID *Thelychiton fleckeri*

Oct–Dec. **ID: Pseudobulbs thin, numerous aerial growths; flowers apricot-coloured to burnt orange, occas. yellow; labellum margins with dense tangled white hairs.** Pseudobulbs to 400 x 4mm. Leaves 2–3, to 80 x 25mm. Racemes to 25mm. Flowers 1–4, 25–30mm across. **Dist.:** Qld (Mt Finnigan to Mt Fisher); 1,000–1,600m alt. Higher peaks on ranges and tlnds on trees and rocks in cloud/mist forest with abundant moisture, humidity and air movement. Very dwarfed plants at high alt. **Status:** Localised, locally common.

BLOTCHED CANE ORCHID *Thelychiton gracilicaulis*

Jul–Oct. **ID: Pseudobulbs cylindrical, yellow/green; leaves dark green, thin-textured; flowers yellow/green (often drooping), large red/brown external blotches (rarely lacking blotches).** Pseudobulbs to 600 x 7mm. Leaves 2–6, to 130 x 40mm. Racemes to 100mm. Flowers 5–30, 10–13mm across. **Dist.:** Qld, NSW (Monto to Gosford); 5–1,000m alt.; also NCal. Coast to ranges; trees and rocks in rainforest, wet sclerophyll forest, moist humid open forest and swamps. **Status:** Widespread, common. **See also:** *T. howeanus, T. nitidus.*

Thelychiton falcorostrus, New England, NSW. L. Copeland   *T. falcorostrus*, Barrington Tops, NSW. D. Banks

Thelychiton finniganensis, Mt Finnigan, Qld. L. Roberts   *T. finniganensis*, Mt Finnigan, Qld. D. Banks

Thelychiton fleckeri, Mt Windsor Tlnd, Qld. D. Banks   *T. fleckeri*, Mt Lewis, Qld. M. Harrison

Thelychiton gracilicaulis, Yabbra, NSW. L. Copeland   *T. gracilicaulis*, Thora, NSW. L. Copeland

OAK ORCHID *Thelychiton jonesii* subsp. *jonesii*
Jul–Oct. **ID: Pseudobulbs spindle-shaped, hard, dark brownish/green, prominently ribbed; flowers cream/white, ageing yellowish; labellum white with purplish marks, tip truncate.** Pseudobulbs to 500 x 40mm. Leaves 2–7, to 150 x 60mm. Racemes to 350mm. Flowers 20–25mm across. **Dist.:** Qld (Iron Ra. to Paluma); 10–1,200m alt. Coast (uncommon) to ranges, tlnds and W slopes; upper branches of rainforest trees; commonest on sheoaks in humid forest. Strong floral scent. Variable sp. **Status:** Widespread, common.

LARGE OAK ORCHID *Thelychiton jonesii* subsp. *magnificus*
Sep–Nov. **ID: Differs from *T. jonesii* subsp. *jonesii* by its larger pseudobulbs (often quite plump), larger leaves, later flowering time, larger whiter flowers with broader sepals and petals and larger labellum.** Flowers 35–50mm across. **Dist.:** Qld (Mt Finnigan to Mt Spec); 1,000–1,600m alt. Higher peaks on rocks and trees in rainforest/mist forest. **Status:** Locally common.

PINK ROCK ORCHID *Thelychiton kingianus*
Aug–Nov. **ID: Pseudobulbs tapered from broad base, often reddish; new shoots pink/red; flowers usually pink, mauve or purplish, occas. white; labellum white to pink/purplish with darker red/purple marks, green central line and 3 ridges.** Pseudobulbs to 500 x 25mm. Leaves 1–6, to 120 x 30mm. Racemes to 200mm. Flowers 3–15, 15–20mm across. **Dist.:** Qld, NSW (Biggenden to Hunter R.); 150–1,200m alt. Coast to ranges. Rocks, boulders, cliffs, and gorges, rarely on base of trees. Small to large, congested clumps with abundant aerial growths. **Status:** Widespread, common.

ATHERTON CANE ORCHID *Thelychiton nitidus*
Jul–Aug. **ID: Similar to *T. gracilicaulis* but with larger brownish/green pseudobulbs and longer racemes with green/yellow flowers, externally uniformly yellowish or red/brown (not blotched).** Pseudobulbs to 900 x 12mm. Leaves 3–7, to 130 x 40mm. Racemes to 300mm. Flowers 14–17mm across. **Dist.:** Qld (Big Tlnd to Mt Fox, W to Undara); 500–1,400m alt. Trees and rocks in rainforest and moist/humid areas in open forest. Flowers pleasantly fragrant. **Status:** Locally common. **See also:** *T. gracilicaulis, T. howeanus*.

Thelychiton jonesii subsp. *jonesii*, Herberton, Qld. J. Roberts

T. jonesii subsp. *magnificus*, Longlands Gap, Qld. D. Banks

T. j. subsp. *jonesii*, McIlwraith Ra, Qld. D. Banks

Thelychiton kingianus, Dooragan, NSW. L. Copeland

T. j. subsp. *m.*, Mt Windsor Tlnd, Qld. M. Harrison

T. kingianus, Werrikimbe, NSW. L. Copeland

Thelychiton nitidus, Upper Barron, Qld. D. Banks

T. nitidus, Ravenshoe, Qld. M. Clements

THE *THELYCHITON SPECIOSUS* GROUP

Popularly known as the 'Dendrobium speciosum complex', this is the most significant group of rock- and tree-dwelling orchids in E Austraila. Recognised by a prolific system of coarse roots, crowded clumps of thick, hard pseudobulbs, each pseudobulb crowned with a group of large, thick, spreading leathery leaves, and long racemes of showy waxy flowers. This variable complex, which consists of a series of vegetative and floral variants, extends from Cape Melville on CYP in NE Qld to Cann R. in East Gippsland, Vic. Extending over some 2,500km, plants of this complex occupy a wide diversity of habitats from coastal sites to the ranges and tlnds, ranging from tropics and subtropics to temperate zones. Two subspecies are recognised.

SYDNEY ROCK ORCHID, ROCK LILY *Thelychiton speciosus* subsp. *speciosus*
Jul–Oct. **ID.: Roots spreading or erect; pseudobulbs mostly tapered, occas. cylindrical; leaves 2–5; flowers white, cream or dull yellow. Dist.** Qld, NSW, Vic (Mt Moffat/ Yeppoon to Cann R.); 0–1,000m alt. Coast to ranges and tlnds, mainly rocks, boulders, cliffs, headlands, less commonly trees; sheltered to exposed positions in various forested habitats. **Notes:** Variable taxon. Although the following components of this complex have previously been recognised as distinct taxa and given formal botanical names at species, subspecies or varietal rank, they are informally grouped here as variants of *T. speciosus* subsp. *speciosus*. These variants can be difficult to define with certainty due genetic variation and the impact of hybridisation.

- *Thelychiton epiphyticus*
Notes: NSW (Illawarra region): 400–700m alt. Grows on trees in tall moist/wet forest, around waterfalls, escarpments and cliff faces; spreading roots, long cylindrical pseudobulbs.

- *Thelychiton tarberi*
Notes: Qld, NSW (Maleny to Mangrove Mtn, inland to Darling Downs): 50–1,200m alt. Trees and rocks in rainforest and moist open forest; erect, litter-trapping roots, cylindrical pseudobulbs, small cream/white flowers.

- *Thelychiton rex*
Notes: Qld (Calliope Ra. to Bunya Mtns): 100–600m alt. Trees and rocks in rainforest and slopes near streams; mixture of erect litter-trapping roots and spreading roots, short to long cylindrical pseudobulbs, large, cream/yellow to bright yellow flowers.

- *Thelychiton capricornicus*
Notes: Qld (Byfield Ra. to Yeppoon to Rockhampton): 50–250m alt. Rock faces of old volcanic plugs; spreading roots, cylindrical pseudobulbs, small white flowers.

T. speciosus subsp. *speciosus*, Central Coast, NSW. M. Harrison

T. s. subsp. *speciosus*, Watagans, NSW. D. Banks

Thelychiton speciosus subsp. *speciosus* (also known as *T. rex*), Kroombit Tops, Qld. D. Banks

T. speciosus subsp. *speciosus* (also known as *T. coriaceus*), Blackdown Tlnd, Qld. M. Harrison

Thelychiton speciosus subsp. *speciosus* (also known as *T. tarberi*), Dove Mtn, NSW. M. Harrison

• *Thelychiton coriaceus*

Notes: Qld (Blackdown Tlnd, Carnarvon Gorge, Mt Moffat): 50–800m alt. Inland from coast. Boulders, escarpments and cliff faces; spreading roots, relatively short tapered pseudobulbs, fleshy, cream/yellow to yellow flowers. New growths dark purplish colour.

RAINFOREST ROCK ORCHID *Thelychiton speciosus* subsp. *curvicaulis*

Jul–Sep. **ID.: Roots spreading; pseudobulbs cylindrical or weakly tapered; leaves 1–3; flowers white, cream or creamy/pale yellow.** Dist. Qld (Cape Melville to Paluma, inland to tlnds); 20–1,200m alt. Coast to ranges and tlnds on rocks, boulders, cliffs and trees in rainforest and humid open forest/woodland. **Notes:** Although the following components of this complex have previously been recognised as distinct taxa and given formal botanical names at species, subspecies or varietal rank, they are informally grouped here as variants of *T. speciosus* subsp. *curvicaulis*. These variants can be difficult to define with certainty due genetic variation and the impact of hybridisation.

• *Thelychiton pedunculatus*

Notes: Qld (Mt Windsor Tlnd, Evelyn Tlnd): 850–1,200m alt. Exposed rocks among forest on W slopes; pseudobulbs short, tapered, leaves thick, leathery, single inflorescence per pseudobulb, long peduncle, small uncrowded flowers.

• *Thelychiton spectabilis*

Notes: Qld (Eungella): 700–1,250m alt. High on trees in mountainous rainforest and tall open forest; also rocks and boulders; long cylindrical pseudobulbs, crowded, large, creamy-yellow to pale yellow flowers.

• *Thelychiton biconvexus*

Notes: Qld (Mt Windsor Tlnd to Mt Finnigan): 700–1,000m alt. Rocks, cliffs and trees in or close to rainforest; spindle-shaped straight or curved pseudobulbs, ellipsoid in cross-section, racemes with long peduncle, white/cream flowers.

• *Thelychiton rupicola*

Notes: Qld (Mt Windsor Tlnd to Mt Elliot): 400–800m alt. Exposed boulders and cliffs at high alt.; relatively short tapered pseudobulbs, racemes with long slender smooth peduncle, small flowers.

Thelychiton speciosus subsp. *curvicaulis*, Cape Hillsborough, Qld. M. Clements

T. speciosus subsp. *curvicaulis* (also known as *T. pedunculatus*), Atherton Tlnd, Qld. G. Walsh

Thelychiton speciosus subsp. *curvicaulis* (also known as *T. spectabilis*), Eungella, Qld. B. Dobson

Thelychiton speciosus subsp. *curvicaulis* (also known as *T. rupicola*), Lamb Ra., Qld. J. Walker

Thelychiton speciosus subsp. *curvicaulis* (also known as *T. rupicola*), Luster Ck, Qld. D. Banks

T. speciosus subsp. *curvicaulis* (also known as *T. biconvexus*), Mt Windsor Tlnd, Qld. D. Banks

GROUP 2: PSEUDOBULBS PENDULOUS, 4-SIDED (TETRAGONAL), WITH THIN BASAL REGION; LEAVES TERMINAL, DARK GREEN; FLOWERS SPIDERY.

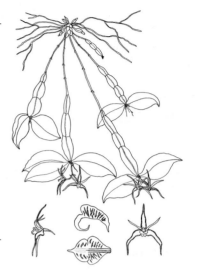

Thelychiton tetragonus

YELLOW TREE SPIDER ORCHID *Thelychiton cacatua*

Jul–Sep. **ID:** Flowers greenish/yellow to pale yellow, occas. with few small marks; labellum white; midlobe narrower than lateral lobes when flattened. Pseudobulbs to 500 x 9mm. Leaves 2–5, to 90 x 25mm. Racemes to 35mm. Flowers 1–4, to 80 x 60mm. Sepals 30–70mm long. **Dist.:** Qld (Mt Windsor Tlnd to Eungella); 600–1,200m alt. Trees in shady sites beside streams and in dense rainforest. Commonest on higher parts of ranges and tlnds. **Status:** Locally common.

BLOTCHED TREE SPIDER ORCHID

Thelychiton capitisyork

Apr–Nov; **ID:** Flowers large, greenish/yellow with prominent red blotches; labellum white with red/purplish lines; midlobe much narrower than lateral lobes when flattened. Pseudobulbs to 600 x 9mm. Leaves 2–5, to 90 x 40mm. Racemes to 35mm. Flowers 1–4, to 120 x 80mm. Sepals 40–70mm long. **Dist.:** Qld (Iron Ra. to Mackay); 0–700m alt. Coast to ranges; trees in streamside vegetation, dense rainforest and rainforest margins. **Status:** Locally common.

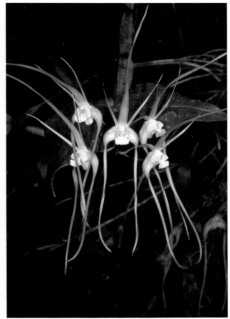

Thelychiton cacatua, Eungella, Qld. M. Harrison

T. cacatua, Mt Windsor Tlnd, Qld. D. Jones

Thelychiton capitisyork, Big Tlnd, Qld. D. Banks

T. capitisyork, Big Tlnd, Qld. M. Harrison

FLARED TREE SPIDER ORCHID *Thelychiton melaleucaphilus*

May–Oct. **ID: Similar to *T. tetragonus* but earlier flowering with larger flowers and broader white labellum with red/purple marks; midlobe as wide as lateral lobes when flattened.** Pseudobulbs to 450 x 9mm. Leaves 2–5, to 90 x 25mm. Racemes to 40mm. Flowers 1–7, to 80 x 40mm. Sepals 40–60mm long. **Dist.:** Qld, NSW (Clarke Ra. to Blue Mtns); 5–600m alt. Coast to ranges. Trees and rocks in rainforest and riverine vegetation; often on paperbarked melaleucas in swamps. **Status:** Sporadic, locally common; endangered (NSW).

BANDED TREE SPIDER ORCHID *Thelychiton tetragonus*

May–Oct. **ID: Flowers scented, green to greenish/yellow with dark red/brown marginal bands; labellum cream/yellowish with dark marks; midlobe narrower than lateral lobes when flattened.** Pseudobulbs to 450 x 9mm. Leaves 1–5, to 80 x 25mm. Racemes to 35mm. Flowers 1–5, to 45 x 40mm. Sepals 20–30mm long. **Dist.:** Qld, NSW (Fraser Is. to Nowra); 5–900m alt. Coast to ranges. Trees in moist shady forests, particularly stream banks, gorges and ravines; occas. rocks. **Status:** Widespread, common.

Thelychiton melaleucaphilus, Iluka, NSW. D. Banks

T. melaleucaphilus flower, Newry SF, NSW. L. Copeland

Thelychiton tetragonus, Royal NP, NSW. M. Harrison

T. tetragonus, Wauchope, NSW. L. Copeland

NAMED NATURAL HYBRIDS

HYBRID ROCK ORCHID *Thelychiton* ×*delicatus*

Aug–Oct. **ID: Sporadic natural hybrid intermediate between** *T. speciosus* [*T. tarberi*] **and** *T. kingianus* **with tapered pseudobulbs and cream/white, pink or mauve flowers; labellum with single ridge.** Pseudobulbs to 600 x 20mm. Leaves to 180 x 35mm. Racemes to 100mm. Flowers 20–25mm across. **Dist.:** Qld, NSW (Toowoomba to Gloucester Bucketts); 250–800m alt. **Notes:** Rocks, boulders, cliff faces and escarpments surrounded by rainforest and humid open forest. Variable flower colour, often externally pink with pale interior.

YELLOW CANE ORCHID *Thelychiton* ×*gracillimus*

Aug–Oct. **ID: Uncommon natural hybrid between a member of the** *T. speciosus* **group, (usually** *T. tarberi*, **less commonly** *T. speciosus*) **and** *T. gracilicaulis* **with narrow pseudobulbs and greenish, cream or yellow flowers.** Pseudobulbs to 600 x 15mm. Leaves to 200 x 60mm. Racemes to 300mm. Flowers 20–25mm across. **Dist.:** Qld, NSW (Maleny to Wauchope); 100–500m alt. **Notes:** Trees and rocks in humid open forest and rainforest margins.

TINAROO CANE ORCHID *Thelychiton* ×*ruppiosus*

Oct–Dec. **ID: Rare natural hybrid between** *T.speciosus* **subsp.** *curvicaulis* [usually *T. pedunculatus* occas. *T. rupicola*] **and** *T. jonesii* **subsp.** *jonesii* **with spindle-shaped pseudobulbs and white/cream flowers; labellum with some purple marks.** Pseudobulbs to 350 x 50mm. Leaves to 150 x 40mm. Racemes to 400mm. Flowers 30–40mm across. **Dist.:** Qld (Atherton Tlnd to Paluma Ra.); 500–800m alt. **Notes:** Trees and rocks in rainforest.

FLUSHED CANE ORCHID *Thelychiton* ×*suffusus*

Aug–Nov. **ID: Natural hybrid between** *T. gracilicaulis* **and** *T. kingianus* **with cylindrical pseudobulbs and white, cream, yellow or pink flowers, externally pink/burgundy; labellum pale yellow with mauve marks.** Pseudobulbs to 250 x 10mm. Leaves to 100 x 40mm. Racemes to 120mm. Flowers 12–15mm across. **Dist.:** Qld, NSW (Kilcoy to Manning R.); 100–800m alt. Mainly on rocks, less commonly trees, in humid open forest and rainforest.

Thelychiton ×*delicatus*, Gloucester, NSW. D. Jones   *Thelychiton* ×*delicatus*, Bulahdelah, NSW. D. Jones

Thelychiton ×*gracillimus*, Coffs Harbour, NSW. R. Tunstall   *T.* ×*gracillimus*, Werrikimbe, NSW. R. Tunstall

Thelychiton ×*ruppiosus*, Mt Fox, Qld. M. Clements

Thelychiton ×*suffusus*, North Brother Mtn, NSW. R. Tunstall   *T.* ×*suffusus*, Hastings R., NSW. E. Rotherham

Genus *Trachyrhizum*

About 9 spp., 1 endemic in Aust.; others in Pacific. Epiphytic clumping orchids with widely spaced narrow pseudobulbs on creeping rhizome, leafy in upper half, and few-flowered racemes arising from lateral buds on pseudobulb opposite a leaf. Flowers generally remain cupped, with thick waxy segments. Growths mature over 2–3 years.

BUTTERCUP ORCHID *Trachyrhizum agrostophyllum*
Jul–Nov. **ID: Pseudobulbs leafy, narrowly cylindrical, tapered to each end; leaves 8–20 per pseudobulb, dark green; flowers somewhat drooping, bright yellow, waxy, fragrant.** Pseudobulbs to 600 x 10mm. Leaves to 100 x 12mm. Racemes to 50mm. Flowers 2–5, 15–20mm across. **Dist.:** Qld (Big Tlnd to Mt Spec); 650–1,600m alt. Ranges and tlnds. Trees and rocks in montane rainforest/mist forest; sheoaks, stunted trees and shrubs with flaky bark on humid ridges and slopes in open forest. **Status:** Widespread, common.

Trachyrhizum agrostophyllum

Dendrobium agrostophyllum, Mt Baldy, Qld. D. Banks

D. agrostophyllum, Mt Lewis, Qld. M. Harrison

Genus *Tropilis*

About 10 spp., 7 endemic in Aust., 3 in NCal. Epiphytic clumping orchids with cylindrical pseudobulbs (ribbed with age) and leathery terminal leaves. Racemes from upper axils carry relatively small flowers with narrow segments. Labellum callus with yellowish wavy ridges. Flowers are basically very similar in most spp., whereas the size and shape of the pseudobulbs is useful for identification. Pseudobulbs either appressed to host or projecting out from host.

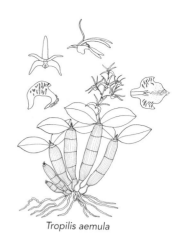

Leaves and pseudobulbs of *Tropilis* spp.

Tropilis aemula

IRONBARK ORCHID *Tropilis aemula*

Aug–Oct. **ID: Pseudobulbs projecting out from host, dumpy or squat, oblong, straight, reddish or purplish/brown; leaves 2–4, thick, leathery, dark green, blunt; flowers, crystalline white; labellum white with purplish marks.** Pseudobulbs to 180 x 12mm. Leaves to 50 x 30mm. Racemes to 60mm. Flowers 2–7, 20–25mm across. **Dist.:** Qld, NSW (Calliope Ra. to Tanja); 10–600m alt. Coast and adjacent ranges on upper trunks and larger branches of ironbarks in open forest, less commonly wetter forest. **Status:** Widespread, locally common.

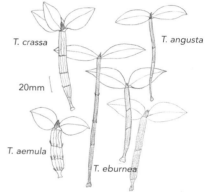

T. crassa

T. angusta

20mm

T. aemula

T. eburnea

T. radiata   *T. eungellensis*

Leaves and pseudobulbs of *Tropilis* species

Tropilis aemula, Yuraygir NP, NSW. L. Copeland

T. aemula, Yuraygir NP, NSW. L. Copeland

123

SLENDER FEATHER ORCHID *Tropilis angusta*

Aug–Oct. **ID: Similar to *T. aemula* but with narrower projecting pseudobulbs; leaves 1–2, also narrower, pointed; racemes longer; flowers larger, white.** Pseudobulbs to 200 x 5mm. Leaves to 60 x 22mm. Racemes to 80mm. Flowers 5–10, 25–38mm across. **Dist.:** Qld, NSW (Lamington Plateau to Whian Whian Ra.); 600–900m alt. Ranges. Trunks and upper branches of large old trees of Forest Oak in wet sclerophyll forest; occas. also on Black Wattle *(Callicoma serratifolia)*. **Status:** Localised, rare.

SKINNY FEATHER ORCHID *Tropilis callitrophilis*

Aug–Sep. **ID: Pseudobulbs projecting, thin, dark plum coloured; leaves 1–2, thin-textured, pointed; flowers opening greenish/yellow with cream centre, quickly becoming apricot-coloured; labellum with purplish bars.** Pseudobulbs to 300 x 3mm. Leaves to 65 x 40mm. Racemes to 25mm. Flowers 1–6, 10–15mm across.
Dist.: Qld (Mt Finnigan to Evelyn Tlnd); 750–1,500m alt. Shrubby myrtles and Stringybark Cypress Pine *(Callitris macleayana)* on slopes and exposed ridgetops in or close to rainforest. **Status:** Highly localised; vulnerable.

Tropilis callitrophilis

SHEOAK FEATHER ORCHID *Tropilis crassa*

Jul–Sep. **ID: Pseudobulbs projecting, thick, dark red/brown; leaves 1–3, thick, leathery, dark green, margins often red, underside purplish; flowers white; labellum white with purplish marks.** Pseudobulbs to 120 x 8mm. Leaves to 60 x 30mm. Racemes to 65mm. Flowers 3–10, 20–30mm across. **Dist.:** Qld (Atherton Tlnd, Mt Spurgeon); 900–1,200m alt. Upper trunks and larger branches of large old Forest Oak trees in moist areas of open forest. **Status:** Highly localised.

Tropilis angusta, Whian Whian, NSW. L. Copeland

T. angusta, Whian Whian, NSW. L. Copeland

Tropilis callitrophilis, Mt Windsor Tlnd, Qld. M. Harrison

T. callitrophillis, Mt Windsor Tlnd, Qld. D. Weise

Tropilis crassa, Mt Spurgeon, Qld. J. Walker

T. crassa, Mt Spurgeon, Qld. J. Walker

RAINFOREST FEATHER ORCHID *Tropilis eburnea*

Aug–Oct. **ID: Pseudobulbs mainly appressed to host, straight, dark reddish/green; leaves 1–2, moderately thick, leathery, dark green, tapered to long sharpish point; flowers opening greenish/cream, ageing to cream; labellum cream with purplish marks.** Pseudobulbs to 120 x 6mm. Leaves to 90 x 30mm. Racemes to 50mm. Flowers 2–7, 16–22mm across. **Dist.:** Qld, NSW (Fraser Is. to near Bega); 10–800m alt. Coast to ranges. Trees in sheltered gullies and moist/wet forest, including rainforest; occas. on rocks. **Status:** Widespread, sporadic.

EUNGELLA IRONBARK ORCHID *Tropilis eungellensis*

Aug–Sep. **ID: Pseudobulbs projecting, straight, hard, dark greenish/brown; leaves 1–3, thick-textured, leathery, dark green, blunt; flowers white; labellum white with purple marks, upper surface densely papillate.** Pseudobulbs to 100 x 8mm. Leaves to 50 x 25mm. Racemes to 50mm. Flowers 3–8, 20–30mm across. **Dist.:** Qld (Paluma Ra., Clarke Ra., Connors Ra.); 600–900m alt. Ranges. Trees, especially ironbarks, on slopes, ridges and gullies in humid open forest. Small clumps of short squat pseudobulbs. **Status:** Localised.

BRUSHBOX FEATHER ORCHID *Tropilis radiata*

Aug–Oct. **ID: Pseudobulbs mainly appressed to host, radiating like wheel spokes, straight, dark reddish/green; leaves 1–3, leathery, dark green; flowers crystalline white; labellum cream/white with purplish marks.** Pseudobulbs to 200 x 8mm. Leaves to 50 x 25mm. Racemes to 100mm. Flowers 5–11, 25–40mm across. **Dist.:** Qld, NSW (Eungella to Wauchope); 10–1,000m alt. Coast to ranges. Scaly basal bark of Brush Box (*Lophostemon confertus*) in moist/wet forest, especially slopes above gullies and streams in ranges. **Status:** Widespread, common.

Tropilis eburnea, Bugong Ck, NSW. A. Stephenson

T. eburnea, Dharug, NSW. M. Clements

Tropilis eungellensis, Eungella, Qld. J. Roberts

T. eungellensis, Eungella, Qld. D. Banks

Tropilis radiata, Brunswick Heads, NSW. D. Banks

T. radiata, Dorrigo, NSW. L. Copeland

THE *VANDA* ALLIANCE

Commonly known as vandaceous orchids or sarcanths, this important group of epiphytes/lithophytes in the tribe Vandeae subtribe Aeridiinae is recognised by its monopodial growth habit in which the main stem is not swollen and is capable of continuous growth from the top. Branching can occur from any node along its length, although most branches seem to arise from lower nodes. Some of the smaller species do not branch much at all. Flower stems arise from nodes on side of main growth, not terminally as in sympodial orchids. In Aust. this group is represented by 25 genera with 58 species on the mainland and 6 in the island territories (4 on Christmas Is., 1 on Lord Howe Is. and 1 on Norfolk Is.).

Leafless species: Some highly specialised members of the subtribe are leafless and the process of photosynthesis is completely taken over by the roots (*Chiloschista, Microtatorchis* and *Taeniophyllum*).

Twig epiphytes: Many of the smaller species of this group commonly grow on the smaller branches and twigs of their host, often towards outer parts of canopy, rarely on larger branches and trunks. Although small, these twig epiphytes usually have an extensive system of long, overlapping and intertwining roots that form a columnar structure along host twigs.

Floral features: The labellum is either hinged to the apex of column foot so that it can pivot under the weight of a pollinator, or else it is immovably fixed to base of column or to sides and apex of the column foot. The labellum usually has a basal spur that is hollow and sac-like and often contains nectar. The labellum midlobe is frequently adorned with hairs or thickened callus-like structures.

Flowering strategies: A number of these orchids have flowers that develop singly or in small groups, each lasting from a few hours to several days before closing and being replaced by the next bud (or buds) which develops in sequence along the raceme (termed sequential flowering or progressive flowering). This results in a series of spasmodic flowerings after which a raceme can end up carrying capsule(s) from earlier flowering events while new buds are developing on the less mature apical part of the inflorescence.

Gregarious flowering also occurs in some species, such as *Brachypeza archytas* and *Bogoria matutina*, whereby all the mature plants in a region open some or all of their flowers simultaneously on the same morning. This flowering event is followed by a non-flowering period until a specific stimulus (such as heavy rain) triggers another massed floral display.

Genus *Bogoria*

Thirteen spp., 1 endemic in Aust., others in PNG, Indon., Solomon Is. Epiphytic orchids with thin smooth roots, sparsely branched stems, large thin-textured leaves and slender racemes with small colourful short-lasting flowers produced synchronously in spasmodic bursts. Labellum hinged. NOTES: Previously placed in *Rhinerrhizopsis*.

FRECKLE ORCHID *Bogoria matutina*

Jul–Sep. **ID: Stem single, semi-pendulous; leaves partially drooping, thin-textured, dark green, usually heavily suffused with pink/mauve; racemes pendulous; flowers cupped, tawny/yellow, heavily marked with brown.** Leaves to 300 x 60mm. Racemes to 450mm. Flowers 10–50, c.15mm across. **Dist.:** Qld (CYP – Iron Ra., McIlwraith Ra.); 200–600m alt. Trees and rocks in humid gallery forest beside streams and on margins of isolated patches of rainforest. Flowers fragrant, lasting few hours. **Status:** Localised; vulnerable.

Bogoria matutina

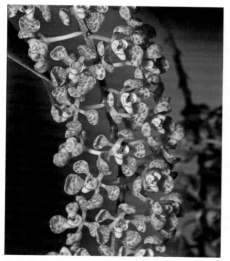

Bogoria matutina, Iron Ra., Qld. M. Clements

Bogoria matutina, Iron Ra., Qld. D. Jones

Genus *Chiloschista*

Three spp., 1 in Aust., 1 in Indon. and 1 in India. Small leafless epiphytic orchids with radiating flat green photosynthetic roots that replace the function of leaves and thin racemes with numerous small short-lasting flowers opening in spasms. Labellum fixed.

Chiloschista phyllorhiza

STARFISH ORCHID *Chiloschista phyllorhiza*
Nov–Feb. **ID: Roots flattened, grey/green roughened, radiating out from inconspicuous central stem; racemes erect to arching, thin; flowers crystalline white with yellow labellum, opening in sporadic groups.** Roots 6–10mm across. Racemes to 150mm. Flowers 10–50, 10–14mm across. **Dist.:** NT (near Darwin), Qld (Torres Strait Is., Cape York to Tully R.); 0–200m alt. Trees in coastal/near-coastal swamps, streamside vegetation, mangroves, rainforest margins, gullies and humid slopes. Flowers fragrant, last for few hours. **Status:** Locally common.

Chiloschista phyllorhiza, Weary Bay, Qld. D. Banks

Chiloschista phyllorhiza, Iron Ra., Qld. M. Clements

Genus *Drymoanthus*

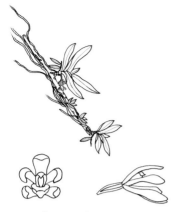

Eight spp., 1 endemic in Aust., 2 in NZ, 5 in NCal. Small epiphytic orchids with relatively thick roots, short stems, few short flat leathery leaves and stubby thick racemes with small short-lasting (1–3 days) greenish flowers. Labellum fixed.

Drymoanthus minutus

GREEN MIDGET ORCHID *Drymoanthus minutus*

Dec–Feb. **ID: Small tufting sp. with coarse roots; stems short, thick (often single); leaves dark green, crowded, leathery; racemes stiff; flowers cupped, greenish with white labellum.** Leaves to 50 x 10mm. Racemes 10–25mm. Flowers 1–7, 2–2.5mm across. **Dist.:** Qld (Cairns to Paluma Ra.); 100–850m alt. Coast to ranges. Trees and shrubs in swamps and beside streams. Can flower when very small. Flowers tiny, fragrant. Disproportionately large capsules often prominent. **Status:** Locally common.

Drymoanthus minutus, Carrington, Qld. J. Fanning

Drymoanthus minutus, Kuranda, Qld. M. Clements

Genus *Luisia*

About 30 spp., 2 in Aust., others in Asia, SE Asia, Polyn., Indon., PNG. Untidy epiphytic orchids with thick roots attached to the host, long straggly fibrous stems, well-spaced tough leathery terete leaves and short club-like inflorescences arising on stems opposite a leaf, producing groups of flowers at intervals, the scape lengthening before each batch of flowers opens. Flowers resupinate, on thick curved stalks, lasting several days, often not opening widely. Labellum fixed.

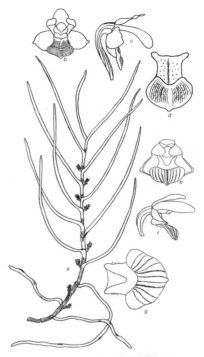

Australian species of Luisia (*L. atacta* a, b, c. d; *L. corrugata* e, f, g)

SMOOTH VELVET ORCHID *Luisia atacta*

Nov–Apr. **ID: Stems semi-pendulous, wiry; leaves rigid, terete, dark green; racemes with numerous overlapping hairless bracts; flowers 1–3 open at sporadic intervals, green with smooth dark burgundy labellum.** Stems to 400mm. Leaves to 200 x 5mm. Racemes 5–15mm. Flowers c.8 x 11mm. **Dist.:** Qld (Thursday Is., Moa Is., Cape York to Daintree R.); 0–200m alt. Trees in coastal/near-coastal rainforest, humid scrub and mangroves. **Status:** Widespread, common.

GROOVED VELVET ORCHID *Luisia corrugata*

Nov–Apr. **ID: Similar to previous sp. but forming larger tangled clumps, racemes with sparsely hairy bracts and slightly smaller green flowers with a red labellum, its surface with radiating grooves or wrinkles.** Flowers c.8 x 9mm. **Dist.:** NT (Melville Is., N coastal parts of NT mainland); 0–50m alt. Rough-barked trees in coastal forest and margins of lowland monsoon rainforest, usually in bright light. **Status:** Highly localised; vulnerable.

Luisia atacta, Big Tlnd, Qld. M. Harrison

L. atacta, Iron Ra., Qld. M. Clements

Luisia corrugata, Melville Is., NT. M. Clements

L. corrugata, Melville Is., NT. D. Jones

Genus *Micropera*

About 12 spp., 1 extending to Aust., others in SE Asia, Malaysia, PNG. Large epiphytic orchids with coarse thick roots, long fibrous stems, widely spaced leathery leaves and short racemes/panicles arising on the stem opposite a leaf and bearing whitish flowers which face outwards or towards apex of raceme. Labellum fixed.

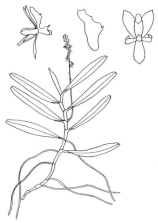

Micropera fasciculata

DISMAL ORCHID *Micropera fasciculata*

Mar–Jun. **ID: Coarse epiphyte with erect to semi-pendulous sparsely branched fibrous stems (lower half usually leafless); leaves green to yellow/green, stiff, leathery; racemes erect, slender; flowers whitish/brownish, usually upside-down.** Stems to 1.2m. Leaves to 150 x 30mm. Racemes to 250mm. Flowers 10–20, to 30 x 15mm. **Dist.:** Qld (Cape York to Townsville); 0–500m alt.; also PNG, Indon. Coast to ranges. Large clumps on trees and rocks in coastal and lowland rainforest. **Status:** Widespread, common.

Micropera fasciculata, Capsize Ck, Qld. D. Jones

M. fasciculata, Iron Ra., Qld. M. Clements

Genus *Microtatorchis*

About 30 spp., 1 endemic in Aust.; others in PNG, Indon., NCal., Philippines, Samoa. Tiny leafless epiphytic orchids with flattened green photosynthetic roots replacing leaves, thin racemes with fleshy zigzagged rachis and small tubular greenish flowers opening singly. Racemes continue growth and flowering for long period. Flowers last 3–5 days. Sepals and petals fused basally with free tips. Labellum fixed. NOTES: Fast-growing orchids often found near the tips of growing shoots. Sometimes included in *Taeniophyllum*.

MT WINDSOR RIBBONROOT *Microtatorchis clementsii*

May–Oct. **ID: Leafless sp. growing singly with flat green roots c.1mm across; racemes flowering progressively and increasing in length; peduncle thread-like, glabrous; rachis thick and fleshy, zigzagged, with bracts in 2 ranks; flowers tubular, pale green, opening singly.** Racemes 10–30mm. Flowers 5–50, c.1.5 x 1mm. **Dist.:** Qld (Mt Windsor Tlnd, Henrietta Creek, Paluma); 1,000–1,250m alt. Tree and shrub branches in highland rainforest. **Status:** Highly localised, readily overlooked.

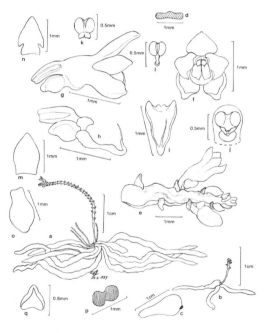

Microtatorchis clementsii, Mt Windsor Tlnd, Qld. M. Clements

Microtatorchis clementsii, Mt Windsor Tlnd, Qld

a. flowering plant; b. young plant with first flower; c. protocorm; d. cross section of root; e. apical part of inflorescence; f. flower from front; g. flower from side; h. column and labellum from side; i. labellum from above; j. column from front; k. anther cap; l. pollinarium; m. dorsal sepal; n. petal; o. lateral sepal; p. cross section of rachis; q. floral bract.

Genus *Mobilabium*

HOOK-LEAF *Mobilabium hamatum*

Jul–Sep. **ID:** Single sp. endemic in Aust. **Small sparse straggly epiphyte with numerous coarse attached and aerial roots; stems 1–few, erect/pendulous; leaves widely spaced, yellow/green, stiff, leathery with hooked tip; flowers opening widely, cream, pale green or brownish with few red/purplish marks; labellum hinged.** Leaves to 70 x 6mm. Racemes 30–60mm. Flowers 5–15, 6–7mm across. **Dist.:** Qld (Big Tlnd near Cooktown to Paluma Ra.); 600–1,300m alt. Ranges and tlnds. Trees and shrubs in wetter humid forest, particularly rainforest. **Status:** Locally common.

Mobilabium hamatum

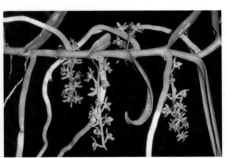

Mobilabium hamatum, Atherton Tlnd, Qld. M. Harrison

Mobilabium hamatum, Koombooloomba, Qld. D. Jones

M. hamatum, Topaz, Qld. R. Tunstall

Genus *Peristeranthus*

BEETLE ORCHID *Peristeranthus hillii*
Aug–Dec. **ID:** Single sp. endemic in Aust.
Moderately large, sparsely branched epiphyte
with coarse attached roots; stem tips upcurved;
leaves spreading with semi-drooping tips; racemes
pendulous; flowers downward-facing, greenish
with crimson-spots; labellum hinged. Leaves to
250 x 40mm. Racemes to 250mm. Flowers 20–70,
5–7mm across. **Dist.:** Qld, NSW (Bloomfield R. to
Port Macquarie); 0–1,100m alt. Coast and adjacent
hills in temperate/subtropical regions, mtns/tlnds
in tropics. Shrubs and trees in rainforest; ridge tops
and humid slopes in drier forest; semi-deciduous
vine thickets. **Status:** Localised; vulnerable.

Peristeranthus hillii

Peristeranthus hillii, Broken Head, NSW. J. Roberts

P. hillii, Iluka, NSW. L. Copeland

137

Genus *Phalaenopsis*

Large diverse genus (c.45 spp.) centred mainly in Asia and Pacific. One endemic sp. in Aust. Small to large epiphytic orchids with long coarse roots, sparsely branched short stems, small to large, leathery, spreading to pendulous leaves (usually widest towards apex) and long racemes/panicles with small to large, widely opening, long-lasting flowers. Labellum fixed.

Phalaenopsis rosenstromii

NATIVE MOTH ORCHID *Phalaenopsis rosenstromii*

Dec–Apr; also sporadic. **ID: Stems short, fibrous; leaves semi-pendulous, dark green, thick, fleshy; panicles arching, sparsely branched; flowers white, flat, moth-like; labellum white with yellow and red/brown streaks.** Leaves to 300 x 70mm. Panicles to 750mm. Flowers 2–10, 50–80mm across. **Dist.:** Qld (CYP – Iron Ra., McIlwraith Ra., Daintree River to Paluma Ra.); 200–500m alt.; also PNG. Trees and occas. rocks in rainforest and wetter humid forest in airy, semi-shady situations; deep gorges; close to waterfalls and streams. **Status:** Highly localised; endangered.

Phalaenopsis rosenstromii, McIlwraith Ra, Qld. J. Walker

P. rosenstromii, McIlwraith Ra, Qld. M. Harrison

Genus *Plectorrhiza*

Five spp., 4 endemic on mainland Aust., *P. erecta* on
Lord Howe Is (page 204). Small to moderate-sized epiphytic
orchids with coarse roots (often tangled), short to relatively
long wiry stems, short leathery leaves and short thin
racemes with few small flowers held out from flower stem
on stalks. Labellum fixed. NOTES: *Plectorrhiza erecta* from
Lord Howe Is. has an upright growth habit. Most spp. with
fragrant flowers. Includes spp. previously placed in genera
Papillilabium and *Schistotylus*.

Plectorrhiza tridentata

IMP ORCHID *Plectorrhiza beckleri*

Sep–Oct. **ID: Small tufted plant with thin wiry roots;
stem short; leaves green with pink/purple spots; racemes
to 40mm long, thin; flowers pale green or brownish with white, green or yellowish
labellum.** Leaves to 50 x 4mm. Racemes to 40mm. Flowers 2–8, 4–6mm across. **Dist.:**
Qld, NSW (Mapleton to Waterfall); 5–800m alt. Coast to ranges. Shrubs and small
trees on slopes above and beside streams; dry humid gullies; sheltered slopes in humid
forest. **Status:** Locally common. Badly impacted by 2019–20 fires. Previously known as
Papilliabium beckleri.

Plectorrhiza beckleri, Wauchope, NSW. L. Copeland

P. beckleri, Black Scrub, NSW. L. Copeland

SMALL TANGLE ORCHID *Plectorrhiza brevilabris*

Nov–Feb. **ID: Straggly epiphyte, often pendulous; roots coarse, wiry; stem flattened; leaves dark green; racemes thin, zigzagged; flowers green to brown with darker brown patches, labellum with prominent white central area.** Stem to 500mm. Leaves to 80 x 15mm. Racemes to 180mm. Flowers 8–10mm across. **Dist.:** Qld (McIlwraith Ra. to Conondale Ra., Caboolture, Noosa); 0–1,300m alt. Coast to ranges and tlnds. Shrubs and small trees in rainforest and twigs of larger trees; rarely on mangroves. Colonises Hoop Pine plantations. **Status:** Widespread, common.

PURPLE SPRITES *Plectorrhiza purpurata*

Aug–Dec. **ID: Small tufted twig epiphyte often suspended by 1-few roots; leaves grey/ green with purple-spots, sharply pointed; racemes very thin, arching to pendulous, flexuous; flowers pale green with purple blotches, labellum white.** Stem 10–30mm. Leaves to 40 x 3mm. Racemes to 40mm. Flowers 4–5mm across. **Dist.:** Qld, NSW (Kenilworth to Barrington Tops); 600–1,100m alt. Ranges and tlnds. Twigs and small branches on shrubs and trees in humid forests and swampy areas; occas. rainforest. **Status:** Localised, uncommon. Badly impacted by 2019/20 fires. Previously known as *Schistotylus beckleri*.

COMMON TANGLE ORCHID, TANGLE ROOT *Plectorrhiza tridentata*

Sep–Jan. **ID: Untidy hanging epiphyte suspended by 1-few long roots; leaves well-spaced, green or purplish; racemes thin, pendulous; flowers green or brown with prominent white labellum, fragrant.** Stem to 300mm. Leaves to 250 x 40mm. Racemes to 120mm. Flowers 6–8mm across. **Dist.:** Qld (N to Mt Windsor Tlnd), NSW (e), Vic (e); 5–1,000m alt. Coast to ranges and tlnds. Shrubs and trees in rainforest, often near or overhanging streams; shady humid forest, gullies, sheltered slopes and swamps; occas. on rocks. Most roots aerial and tangled. **Status:** Widespread, common.

Plectorrhiza brevilabris, Mt Windsor Tlnd, Qld. M. Harrison   *P. brevilabris*, Mt Windsor Tlnd, Qld. M. Clements

Plectorrhiza purpurata, Dorrigo, NSW. D. Banks   *P. purpurata*, Cottan-Bimbang NP, NSW. L. Copeland

Plectorrhiza tridentata, Yabbra, NSW. L. Copeland   *P. tridentata*, Cottan-Bimbang NP, NSW. L. Copeland

141

Genus *POMATOCALPA*

Diverse genus of c.60 spp. centred on Asia and Pacific. Two in Aust., 1 endemic. Epiphytic orchids with coarse spreading roots, fibrous leafy stems, leathery spreading leaves and erect/pendulous multiflowered racemes/panicles carrying small long-lived flowers pointing towards the inflorescence apex. Labellum fixed.

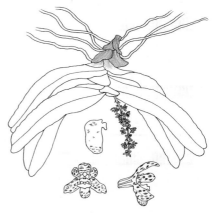

Pomatocalpa macphersonii

BLOTCHED SARCANTH

Pomatocalpa macphersonii

Jul–Oct. **ID: Relatively small single-growth epiphyte with thick cord-like roots; stem flattish; leaves dark green, stiff, main vein ridged beneath; racemes stiffly decurved; flowers yellow with red blotches, cupped.** Stem to 100mm. Leaves to 250 x 35mm. Racemes to 40mm. Flowers 3–30, 7–10mm across. **Dist.:** Qld (Cape York to Rockhampton); 0–600m. Coast to ranges. Rainforest trees, especially in lowlands. Plants often at right angles to host. **Status:** Widespread, common.

POUCHED SARCANTH *Pomatocalpa marsupiale*

Nov–May. **ID: Robust clumping epiphyte with numerous thick roots; stems upright, thick; leaves numerous, yellow/green, strap-like, arching; panicles stiffly erect, each branch with 15–20 densely crowded, upward-facing green/brown flowers with yellowish labellum.** Stems to 500mm. Leaves to 300 x 50mm. Panicles to 450mm. Flowers c.15mm across. **Dist.:** Qld (CYP – Iron Ra., McIlwraith Ra.); 10–600m alt; also PNG. Coast to ranges. Upper canopy of trees along stream banks and open situations in rainforest; occas. exposed rocks in rainforest. **Status:** Highly localised.

Pomatocalpa macphersonii, Cape Tribulation, Qld. A. Locke   *P. macphersonii*, McIlwraith Ra., Qld. A. Locke

Pomatocalpa marsupiale, Iron Ra., Qld. D. Banks   *P. marsupiaule*, Iron Ra., Qld. M. Clements

Genus *Rhinerrhiza*

RASPY ROOT ORCHID *Rhinerrhiza divitiflora*
Aug–Nov. **ID:** Single sp. endemic in Aust. **Single-growth epiphyte with flat grey warty roots 4–6mm across; leaves parchment-like, dark green, margins wavy; racemes pendulous; flowers spidery, short-lasting (1–2 days), yellow/orange with red blotches; labellum white, hinged.** Leaves to 150 x 30mm. Racemes to 300mm. Flowers 10–60, c.40–50mm across. **Dist.:** Qld, NSW (Atherton Tlnd to Berowra Waters); 0–1,200m alt. Coast to mountains and tlnds in drier rainforest, gorges, gullies and moist humid areas in open forest. Flowers open in spasmodic groups. **Status:** Widespread, common.

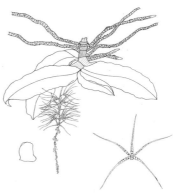

Rhinerrhiza divitiflora

Rhinerrhiza divitiflora, Mt Binga, Qld. J. Roberts

R. divitiflora, Kippaxs, NSW. D. Banks

Genus *Robiquetia*

About 20 spp., 2 in Aust., 1 endemic; others in India, Malaysia, Philippines, Indon., PNG. Large epiphytic orchids with thick smooth roots, fibrous stems, large leathery leaves and long decurved to pendulous multiflowered racemes carrying moderately small flowers that often face towards apex of raceme. Labellum fixed.

Robiquetia gracilistipes

LARGE POUCHED ORCHID *Robiquetia gracilistipes*

Mar–May. **ID:** Coarse straggly epiphyte, usually with a single main pendulous growth, tip upturned; leaves numerous, yellow/green, thick, leathery; racemes stiffly pendulous; flowers cream, pale green or brownish with red spots. Stem 300–1,500mm. Leaves to 250 x 60mm. Racemes to 300mm. Flowers 10–40, 6–7mm across. **Dist.:** Qld (Iron Ra. to Paluma Ra.); 0–800m alt.; also PNG. Coast to ranges. Rocks and trees in rainforest, often near streams; rarely in mangroves. Can form large untidy clumps. **Status:** Widespread, common.

GREEN POUCHED ORCHID *Robiquetia wassellii*

Jun–Aug. **ID:** Sparse clumping epiphyte with pendulous stems, growing tips upcurved; leaves parchment-like, dark green; racemes stiffly decurved; flowers crowded, dark green with pink/red central areas and white/yellowish labellum spur. Stems to 500mm. Leaves to 140 x 30mm. Racemes to 150mm. Flowers 20–50, c.14 x 6mm. **Dist.:** Qld (CYP – Iron Ra., McIlwraith Ra.); 200–600m alt. Lowland hills and ranges. Trees and boulders on shady slopes and humid gullies in rainforest. **Status:** Locally common.

Robiquetia gracilistipes, Station Ck, Qld. M. Harrison

R. gracilistipes, Iron Ra., Qld. D. Titmuss

Robiquetia wassellii, McIlwraith Ra., Qld. D. Jones

R. wassellii, McIlwraith Ra., Qld. R. Tunstall

Genus *Saccolabiopsis*

About 14 spp., 2 endemic in Aust.; others in Asia and Pacific. Small epiphytic orchids with thin smooth roots, short sparsely branched stems, thin-textured leaves and deflexed to pendulous narrow racemes with small greenish flowers facing towards apex of raceme. Labellum fixed.

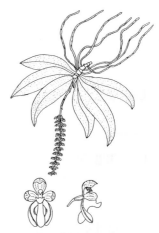

SPOTTED PITCHER ORCHID *Saccolabiopsis armitii*
Sep–Dec. **ID: Small single-growth epiphyte; leaves green/bronze, often with darker spotting; racemes stiffly pendulous; flowers cupped, yellow/green with red marks, white labellum and red anther.** Stem 20–50mm. Leaves to 60 x 12mm. Racemes to 90mm. Flowers 20–50, 3–4mm across. **Dist.:** Qld (Weipa, Bamaga to Bundaberg, inland at Forty Mile Scrub); 0–800m alt. Coast to ranges and up to 200km inland on shrubs and trees, rarely rocks, in drier open humid habitats. Flowers open in spasmodic groups. **Status:** Fragmented, locally common.

Saccolabiopsis armitii

TINY PITCHER ORCHID *Saccolabiopsis rectifolia*
Jun–Aug. **ID: Tiny single-growth epiphyte with thin roots; stem unbranched; leaves thin-textured, light green/yellowish; racemes stiffly projecting away (widening towards apex); flowers cupped, green, labellum white with purple-spots.** Stem 1–15mm. Leaves to 40 x 10mm. Racemes 20–60mm. Flowers 4–15, c.3 x 2mm. **Dist.:** Qld (Russell R. to Johnstone R.); 100–400m alt. Lowlands, hills and ranges. Twigs and smaller outer branches of trees, especially those overhanging streams in rainforest. Easily overlooked. **Status:** Highly localised.

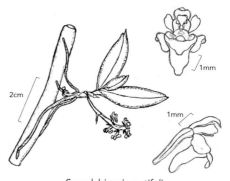

Saccolabiopsis rectifolia

Saccolabiopsis armitii, 40 Mile Scrub, Qld. J. Walker

S. armittii, Dan Dan Scrub, Qld. D. Banks

Saccolabiopsis rectifolia, Johnstone R., Qld. D. Jones

S. rectifolia, Palmerston NP, Qld. D. Jones

Genus *Sarcanthopsis*

About 7 spp., 1 extending to Aust.; others in Indon., Vanuatu, Fiji, Solomon Is. PNG. Large to very large epiphytic orchids with coarse cord-like spreading roots, thick upright stems covered with fibrous leaf bases, large leathery leaves and panicles carrying globose flowers. Labellum fixed.

Sarcanthopsis warocqueana

GOLIATH ORCHID *Sarcanthopsis warocqueana*
Apr–Aug. **ID: Large straggly/scrambling epiphyte with thick branching stems; leaves spreading, green to yellow/green, strap-shaped; panicles sturdy, each branch with 5–15 yellowish or greenish flowers with red/purple/brown spots.** Stems 1–3m. Leaves to 400 x 70mm. Panicles 150–300mm. Flowers 20–30mm across. **Dist.:** Qld (Moa Is.); 0–100m alt.; also PNG, Solomon Is., Vanuatu, Fiji, Caroline Is. Mainly coastal. Upper branches of trees in rainforest, swamps and close to the sea, usually exposed to full sun. Single juvenile plant collected on Moa Is. **Status:** Highly localised.

Sarcanthopsis warocqueana,
Vanuatu, M. Clements

Genus *Sarcochilus*

About 22 spp., 18 endemic in Aust., 3 or 4 spp. in NCal. Small to medium-sized epiphytes or clumping lithophytes with spreading smooth roots, short fibrous stems covered with persistent leaf bases, relatively small to large leaves and short to long racemes of narrow to rounded flowers, often colourful. Labellum hinged. ID: Look for clumping habit on rocks or epiphytic on trees; leaf features such as size, shape, thickness, margins smooth or toothed, colour and markings, ageing black or not; raceme features such as length, shape, thickness, pendulous or not; flower shape, size and colour.

Sarcochilus falcatus

SARCOCHILUS IS DIVIDED INTO 5 GROUPS

GROUP 1: EPIPHYTES WITH FLAT LEAVES; FLOWERS ROUND IN GENERAL SHAPE.

ORANGE BLOSSOM ORCHID *Sarcochilus falcatus*

Jun–Nov. **ID:** Single-stemmed or clumping epiphyte; leaves curved, dark green, margins finely toothed; racemes arching/pendulous; flowers cream/white, fragrant; labellum with orange/yellow patches overlaid with red/purple stripes. Stems 30–60mm. Leaves to 100 x 12mm. Racemes 50–100mm. Flowers 1–12, 12–30(–45)mm across. **Dist.:** Qld (N to Cooktown), NSW (e), Vic (e); 1–1,400m alt. Coast to mountains and tlnds (only above c.800m in tropics) on trees and rocks in rainforest and moist/humid wetter forests with buoyant air movement. Old leaves turn black. Variable sp. **Status:** Widespread, common; endangered (Vic).

Sarcochilus falcatus, Mt Wilson, NSW. D. Banks

S. falcatus, Koreelah NP, NSW. L. Copeland

LARGE WHITE SARCOCHILUS, SNOWY SARCOCHILUS *Sarcochilus niveus*

Oct–Dec. **ID: Flowering 6–8 weeks later than** *S. falcatus* **and with larger clumps, strongly curved leaves and larger snowy white fragrant flowers; labellum with pale yellow patches and few thin brownish streaks.** Stem 5–80mm. Leaves to 160 x 20mm. Racemes 70–180mm. Flowers 5–15, to 50 x 50mm. **Dist.:** Qld, NSW (Toowoomba to Dorrigo); 50–1,000m alt. Rainforest trees, humid sheltered slopes and beside streams in wetter forest. Commonest on misty mountainous ridgetops; occas. lowland, rarely coastal. **Status:** Sporadic: locally common.

BLOTCHED BUTTERFLY ORCHID *Sarcochilus weinthalii*

Aug–Oct. **ID: Stem single, short; leaves thin textured, green to yellow/green; racemes arching/pendulous; flowers 12–15mm across, cream, white or greenish with large purple/reddish spots/blotches, dark spot on labellum apex.** Leaves to 90 x 12mm. Racemes 50–70mm. Flowers 3–15, 12–15mm across. **Dist.:** Qld, NSW (Bunya Mtns to Richmond R.); 300–700m alt. Hills and ranges well inland from coast. Twigs and small branches of shrubs and small trees in rainforest and wetter forests; isolated patches of dry scrub. **Status:** Highly localised; vulnerable.

GROUP 2: CLUMPING LITHOPHYTES WITH CHANNELLED, THICK-TEXTURED, LEATHERY LEAVES; FLOWERS ROUND IN GENERAL SHAPE

SMALL BOULDER ORCHID *Sarcochilus aequalis*

Aug–Oct. **ID: Stems suberect, sparsely branching; leaves yellow/green; racemes arching, rachis and peduncle of similar length; flowers cream with red/brown central spots; labellum with red bars.** Stems to 200mm. Leaves to 200 x 20mm. Racemes to 120mm. Flowers 5–12, 20–25mm across. **Dist.:** NSW (Dorrigo Plateau, Carrai Plateau, Macleay R. to Manning R.); 400–1,200m alt. Ranges and tlnds. Boulders, cliff faces and rocky escarpments on sheltered slopes in humid forest and near streams. **Status:** Highly localised; endangered. **See also:** *S. hartmannii.*

Sarcochilus niveus, Lamington NP, Qld. L. Copeland

S. niveus, Border Ra., NSW. L. Copeland

Sarcochilus weinthalii, Toonumbar, NSW. L. Copeland

S. weinthalii, Toowoomba, Qld. D. Banks

S. weinthalii, Toowoomba, Qld. D. Titmuss

Sarcochilus aequalis, Oxley Wild Rivers NP, NSW. L. Copeland

S. aequalis, Oxley Wild Rivers NP, Smalls Ck.

S. aequalis, Oxley Wild Rivers NP, NSW. L. Copeland

RAVINE ORCHID *Sarcochilus fitzgeraldii*

Oct–Nov. **ID:** Stems arching/pendulous, freely branching; leaves dark green; racemes arching/pendulous; flowers white with varying degrees of central red/purple/mauve spotting; labellum with red markings and yellow chin. Stems to 500mm. Leaves to 200 x 15mm. Racemes to 200mm. Flowers 4–15, 25–30mm across. **Dist.:** Qld, NSW (Maleny to Carrai); 400–800m alt. Hills and ranges. Boulders in moist ravines, gorges, cliff faces and stream banks in dense rainforest. **Status:** Highly localised; vulnerable (NSW); endangered (Qld).

LARGE BOULDER ORCHID *Sarcochilus hartmannii*

Sep–Nov. **ID:** Stems upright, freely branching; leaves green to yellow/green; racemes erect/arching, peduncle much longer than rachis; flowers white with red central spots; labellum with red bars. Stems to 800mm. Leaves to 200 x 20mm. Racemes to 250mm. Flowers 5–25, 25–30mm across. **Dist.:** Qld, NSW (Toowoomba to Clarence R.); 500–1,000m alt. Ranges and tlnds. Volcanic boulders, cliff faces and escarpments surrounded by forest, in dappled shade to nearly full sun; rarely epiphytic on fibrous-barked tree trunks. **Status:** Localised, sporadic. **See also:** *S. aequalis.*

GROUP 3: SMALL EPIPHYTES WITH SINGLE SHORT STEM; LEAVES FLAT; FLOWERS ANGULAR, OFTEN LONGER THAN WIDE.

BUTTERFLY ORCHID, GUNN'S TREE ORCHID *Sarcochilus australis*

Oct–Jan. **ID:** Leaves strongly curved, dark green; racemes pendulous; flowers scented, green to yellow/green or brownish; labellum white, side lobes usually yellowish with red/purple streaks. Stems 20–50mm. Leaves to 80 x 14mm. Racemes to 160mm. Flowers 2–14, 12–15mm across. **Dist.:** NSW (N to Tenterfield), Vic, Tas; 0–1,000m alt. Coast to ranges on shrubs and trees (occas. rocks) in shady or brightly lit situations in rainforest and other moist/wet humid forests with buoyant air movement; drier thickets and drier rainforest. Often on twigs and smaller branches. **Status:** Widespread, sporadic, locally common.

Sarcochilus fitzgeraldii, Limpinwood NR, NSW. L. Copeland   *S. fitzgeraldii*, Limpinwood NR, NSW. L. Copeland

Sarcochilus hartmannii, Numinbah Valley, Qld. D. Banks   *S. hartmannii*, Lamington NP, Qld. D. Banks

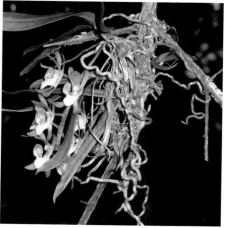

Sarcochilus australis, Dorrigo, NSW. L. Copeland   *S. australis*, Kurrajong Heights, NSW. D. Banks

NORTHERN LAWYER ORCHID *Sarcochilus borealis*

Jun–Dec. **ID:** Leaves dark green, thin-textured, stiffly spreading; flowers green to yellow/green; labellum white with red marks (occas. heavily stained with red). Stems to 80mm. Leaves to 150 x 40mm. Racemes to 140mm. Flowers 2–12, 15–20mm across. **Dist.:** Qld (Mt Windsor Tlnd, Mt Lewis to Toowoomba); 400–1,000m alt. Trees and vines in rainforest and humid slopes in wetter forest close to streams. **Status:** Widespread, common.

BROWN BUTTERFLY ORCHID *Sarcochilus dilatatus*

Aug–Mar. **ID:** Leaves thin textured, dark green, network of reddish lines, sometimes black-spotted; racemes stiff; flowers brown to red/brown (rarely yellowish), opening sporadically; labellum white with yellow/orange marks and red/brown lines. Stems to 30mm. Leaves to 60 x 10mm. Racemes to 70mm. Flowers 2–12, 15–25mm across. **Dist.:** Qld, NSW (Carnarvon Gorge to Nymboida); 0–400m alt. Coast to low ranges. Twigs and small branches of shrubs and trees in drier rainforest, humid slopes, ridges and gorges. Flowers last 3–4 days. **Status:** Sporadic, locally common; endangered (NSW).

HARLEQUIN ORCHID *Sarcochilus hirticalcar*

Nov–Dec. **ID:** Leaves bright green; racemes pendulous; flowers cream to bright yellow, prominently banded with purple/brown to red/brown; labellum hairy, white or yellow with red/brown band. Stems to 100mm. Leaves to 120 x 15mm. Racemes to 60mm. Flowers 2–18, 10–12mm across. **Dist.:** Qld (CYP – McIlwraith Ra.); 300–600m alt. Hills and ranges. Small branches and twigs in riverine forest near small streams and drainage lines. Long-lasting flowers open 1–3 sequentially along racemes. **Status:** Highly localised; vulnerable.

SOUTHERN LAWYER ORCHID *Sarcochilus olivaceus*

Oct–Dec. **ID:** Leaves dark green, thin-textured but stiff; racemes thin; flowers bright green to yellow/green; labellum green/cream to green with red/brown bars and marks. Stems to 80mm. Leaves to 150 x 35mm. Racemes to 140mm. Flowers 2–12, 20–25mm across. **Dist.:** Qld, NSW (Maleny to Mumbulla Mtn); 0–800m alt. Coast to ranges. Rocks, trees and vines in gullies and sheltered slopes near small streams in shady humid forest; often mossy bark of small trees and vines. **See also:** *S. parviflorus*. **Status:** Widespread, common.

Sarcochilus borealis, Eungella, Qld. D. Banks

S. borealis, Mt Baldy, Qld. D. Banks

Sarcochilus dilatatus, Nymboida, NSW. L. Copeland

S. dilatatus, Kroombit Tops, Qld. D. Banks

Sarcochilus hirticalcar, McIlwraith Ra., Qld. A. Stephenson

S. hirticalcar, McIlwraith Ra., Qld. M. Harrison

Sarcochilus olivaceus, Dorrigo, NSW. L. Copeland

S. olivaceus, Ellenborough Falls, NSW. D. Banks

SMALL LAWYER ORCHID *Sarcochilus parviflorus*

Sep. **ID:** Similar to *S. olivaceus* but earlier flowering and with much smaller plants and smaller greenish/brownish flowers which have a vivid white labellum with prominent red bands. Stems to 20mm. Leaves to 70 x 15mm. Racemes to 70mm. Flowers 7–8mm across. **Dist.:** Qld (se), NSW (near Grafton); 5–50m alt. Lowlands. Trees in dry rainforest near streams. **See also:** *S. olivaceus.* **Status:** Highly localised; critically endangered.

BANDED BUTTERFLY ORCHID *Sarcochilus serrulatus*

Aug–Jan. **ID: Stem semi-pendulous; leaves green, curved, thin-textured but leathery, margins wavy and finely toothed; racemes club-shaped; flowers red/brown with white and yellow bands on labellum.** Stem to 20mm. Leaves to 100 x 20mm. Racemes to 40mm. Flowers 12–15mm across. **Dist.:** Qld (Mt Windsor Tlnd to Evelyn Tlnd, Cardwell Ra.); 800–1,300m alt. Ranges and tlnds. Shrubs, trees and vines in dense highland rainforest and beside small streams. Usually in shade. **Status:** Highly localised.

SMALL BUTTERFLY ORCHID *Sarcochilus spathulatus*

Jul–Oct. **ID: Leaves green, thin-textured but leathery, occas. numerous purple spots; racemes pendulous; flowers widely spaced, green, green/brown or brown (rarely yellow), opening sequentially; labellum cream/white with purple marks and yellow tip.** Stems to 40mm. Leaves to 70 x 17mm. Racemes to 50mm. Flowers 1–8, 10–14mm across. **Dist.:** Qld, NSW (Bunya Mtns to Watagan Mtns); 200–1,000m alt. Mainly in mountains, rarely in lowlands. Shrubs, trees and vines in rainforest, wetter forest and scrub; humid slopes in drier rainforest. Often on twigs and smaller branches. **Status:** Widespread, locally common.

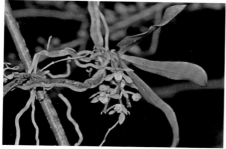

Sarcochilus parviflorus, Chambigne, NSW. L. Copeland

S. parviflorus, Chambigne, NSW. L. Copeland

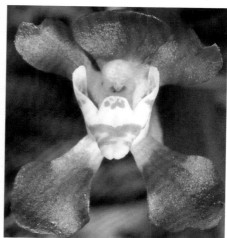

Sarcochilus serrulatus, Mt Lewis, Qld. D. Banks

S. serrulatus, photo of flower from type plant. J. Fanning

Sarcochilus spathulatus, Washpool NP, NSW. L. Copeland

S. spathulatus, Washpool NP, NSW. L. Copeland

GROUP 4: SMALL CLUMPING EPIPHYTES WITH SHORT STEMS and DROOPING NARROW CHANNELLED LEAVES; RACEMES SHORT, THIN; FLOWERS SMALL, OPENING SEQUENTIALLY, FEW OPEN AT ONCE; LABELLUM HAIRY.

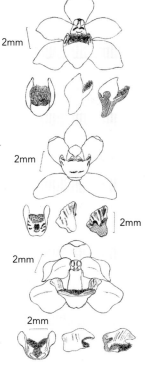

Sarcochilus hillii group; flower from front labellum rear view, from side and longitudinal section. Top *S. hillii*, middle *S. loganii*, bottom *S. tricalliatus*.

MYRTLE BELLS *Sarcochilus hillii*

Oct–Jan. ID: Leaves green, pink or reddish, spotted; flowers white or pale pink, small gap between lateral sepals and petals; labellum white or pink with internal purple stripes and 3 bright yellow calli, densely hairy. Stems to 50mm. Leaves to 100 x 3mm. Racemes to 120mm. Flowers 2–10, 8–10mm across. **Dist.:** Qld, NSW (Rockhampton to Mumbulla Mtn); 0–1,000m alt. Coast to ranges. Trees and rocks on humid slopes, streams and gullies in relatively dry forest. Grey Myrtle is favoured host in NSW. Few flowers open at once. **Status:** Widespread, common.

WONGI FAIRY BELLS *Sarcochilus loganii*

Aug–Sep. ID: Leaves fleshy, dark green; flowers white, lightly scented, large gap between lateral sepals and petals; labellum cream to pale yellow with dark pink marks, inner surface covered with stiff hairs, single domed callus. Stems to 30mm. Leaves to 120 x 4mm. Racemes to 80mm. Flowers 2–8, 6.5– 8.5mm across. **Dist.:** Qld (Mt Walsh NP); 500–700m alt. Hills and ranges. Twig epiphyte on rainforest trees. 1–3 flowers open at once. **Hab.:** Highly localised; endangered.

PALE FAIRY BELLS *Sarcochilus tricalliatus*

Nov–Feb. ID: Leaves green, pink or reddish, spotted; flowers white, no gap between lateral sepals and petals; labellum white with narrow pink/red or purple internal stripes, covered with short glandular hairs, bilobed central callus and 2 smaller calli. Stems to 25mm. Leaves to 100 x 5mm. Racemes to 60mm. Flowers 2–8, 8–10mm across. **Dist.:** Qld (McIlwraith Ra., Cooktown to Rockhampton, inland at Forty Mile Scrub); 200–800m alt. Lowlands to ranges and extending well inland. Rough scaly-barked trees in drier rainforest, vine thickets and stunted trees in gorges. **Status:** Sporadic, uncommon.

Sarcochilus hillii, Picton, NSW. D. Banks

S. hillii, Hortons Ck, NSW. L. Copeland

Sarcochilus loganii, Brooweena, Qld. D. Jones

S. loganii, Mt Walsh, Qld. D. Banks

Sarcochilus tricalliatus, near Charters Towers, Qld. M. Clements

S. tricalliatus, 40 Mile Scrub, Qld. R. Tunstall

GROUP 5: SMALL CLUMPING LITHOPHYTES WITH ERECT TO ARCHING, BROADLY CHANNELLED, FLESHY LEAVES; RACEMES LONG, THIN, ERECT TO ARCHING; FLOWERS SMALL, UPWARD-FACING, CUPPED, OPENING SEQUENTIALLY; LABELLUM HAIRY.

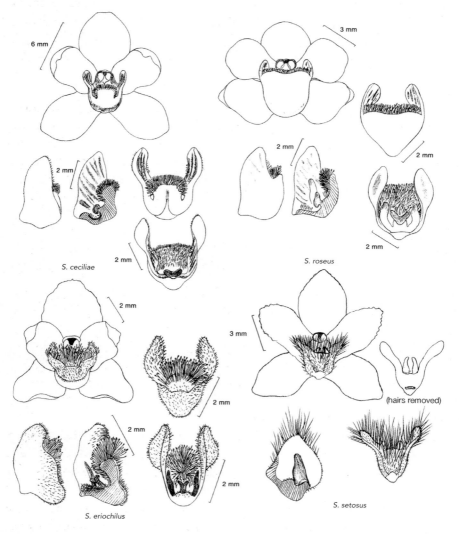

Sarcochilus ceciliae group; flower from front labellum front view, rear view, side view and longitudinal section

Sarcochilus ceciliae, Coongara Rock, Qld. J. Roberts

S. ceciliae, Kroombit Tops, Qld. M. Harrison

FAIRY BELLS *Sarcochilus ceciliae*

Oct–Mar. **ID: Leaves reddish/green, pinkish or brownish, usually with dark wart-like spots; flowers pink; labellum with darker pink irregular bands, single callus; lateral lobes and midlobe separate.** Stems to 80mm. Leaves to 120 x 10mm. Racemes to 200mm. Flowers 3–18, 8–14mm across. **Dist.:** Qld (Atherton Tlnd to Bundaberg); 300–900m alt. Hills and ranges. Crevices and sites of litter accumulation in rocks, boulders and cliff faces in shade to full sun. Flowers last 5–7 days. **Status:** Localised.

Sarcochilus eriochilus, New England, NSW. L. Copeland

S. eriochilus, New England, NSW. L. Copeland

SOUTHERN FAIRY BELLS *Sarcochilus eriochilus*

Nov–Mar. **ID: Leaves reddish/green or brownish, often dark wart-like spots; flowers pale pink (rarely white); labellum pale pink, 3 calli (short central callus and 2 elongate calli); lateral lobes and midlobe separate.** Stems to 120mm. Leaves to 120 x 5mm. Racemes to 200mm. Flowers 3–15, 4–7mm across. **Dist.:** Qld, NSW (Gympie to Manning R.); 300–1,000m alt. Hills and ranges. Boulders, cliff faces and gorges in sun or shade; stony rubble and patches of drier soil on ridge tops; rarely epiphytic on exposed roots and trunk bases. **Status:** Widespread, locally common.

NORTHERN FAIRY BELLS *Sarcochilus roseus*

Oct–Jan. **ID: Plants often with stilt roots; leaves green or pinkish/brown, not spotted; flowers bright rosy pink; labellum with red veins, 3 calli (lobed central callus and 2 elongate calli); lateral lobes fused with midlobe.** Stems to 60mm. Leaves to 80 x 8mm. Racemes to 150mm. Flowers 3–20, 8–10mm across. **Dist.:** Qld (Mt Lewis, Mt Molloy to Atherton Tlnd); 900–1,300m alt. Ranges and tlnds. Cliffs, escarpments, rocks exposed roots and trunk bases in brightly lit to exposed sunny positions. **Status:** Highly localised; vulnerable.

BRISTLY BELLS *Sarcochilus setosus*

Oct–Mar. **ID: Leaves dark green, not spotted; flowers bright pink; petals often toothed; labellum white, covered with long needle-like white hairs to 1.5mm long, 2 calli, elongate; lateral lobes and midlobe separate.** Stems to 80mm. Leaves to 70 x 7mm. Racemes to 150mm. Flowers 3–20, 10–16mm across. **Dist.:** Qld (near Ravenshoe); 600–700m alt. Ranges. Sheltered sites among shrubs and under trees on granite boulders. Propagates by small aerial growths on inflorescences. **Status:** Highly localised; vulnerable.

Genus *Schoenorchis*

About 20 spp., 2 extending to Aust.; others in Asia, SE Asia, Indon., PNG. Small epiphytic orchids with numerous thin roots and narrow stems, narrow to broad, linear or terete leaves and racemes/panicles carrying tiny tubular flowers with overlapping tepals. Labellum fixed.

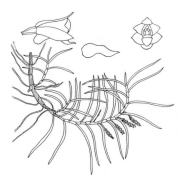

Schoenorchis micrantha

TANGLED FLEA ORCHID *Schoenorchis micrantha*

Apr–Jul. **ID: Tangled clumps; stems curved, twisted, branching; leaves numerous, narrow, green or purplish, curved, fleshy, deeply grooved; racemes stiffly decurved; flowers tiny, densely crowded, tubular to bell-shaped, white.** Stems to 150mm. Leaves 3–6mm long. Racemes to 30mm. Flowers 5–30, c.2mm long. **Dist.:** Qld (Iron Ra. to Tully R.); 0–400m alt.; also PNG. Coast to hills and low ranges. Mangroves and rainforest trees in brightly lit humid situations. Leaves turn reddish in bright light. **Status:** Locally common.

Sarcochilus roseus, Luster Ck, Qld. G. Walsh

S. roseus, Mt Lewis, Qld. M. Harrison

Sarcochilus setosus, Tully Falls, Qld. G. Walsh

S. setosus, Tully Falls, Qld. M. Harrison

Schoenorchis micrantha, McIlwraith Ra., Qld. M. Harrison

S. micrantha, Iron Ra., Qld. D. Banks

FLESHY FLEA ORCHID *Schoenorchis sarcophylla*

Aug–Sep. **ID: Stem single, short, tip upcurved, old parts covered by overlapping bracts; leaves dark green, fleshy, channelled; racemes stiff; flowers tiny, white, tubular (facing end of raceme).** Stem to 50mm. Leaves to 30 x 5mm. Racemes to 40mm. Flowers 5–30, c.3mm long. **Dist.:** Qld (CYP – Iron Ra., McIlwraith Ra.); 400–600m alt.; also PNG. Known from only two localities. Hills and ranges. Twigs on outer canopy of trees overhanging streams; shrubs on humid sheltered ridge. Easily overlooked. **Status:** Highly localised, rare; vulnerable.

Schoenorchis sarcophylla, Palmerston, Qld. M. Harrison   *S. sarcophylla*, McIlwraith Ra., Qld. M. Clements

Genus *Taeniophyllum*

Large diverse genus of c.170 spp. centred on Asia and Pacific. Thirteen named spp. in Aust., including *T. fornicatum* and *T. pusillum* on Christmas Is. (page 216) and *T. norfolkianum* on Norfolk Is. (page 210). Small leafless epiphytic orchids with green roots (photosynthetic), vestigial stems and thin glabrous or hairy racemes with differentiated peduncle and rachis, the continually growing rachis flowering intermittently; flowers small, 1–3 open at once, often tubular with spreading tips, lasting 1–3 days. Labellum fixed. NOTES: Buds, flowers and fruiting capsules can be present on an inflorescence at one time. ID: Look for roots appressed to host or aerial, root shape in cross section (round, flat or triangular), root colour and width; raceme thickness, glabrous/hairy; flower shape (wholly tubular, tubular base with spreading tips, widely opening), colour; spur alignment relative to ovary.

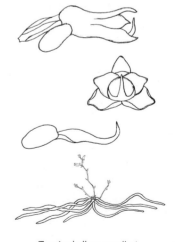

Taeniophyllum muelleri

TAENIOPHYLLUM IS DIVIDED INTO 2 GROUPS

GROUP 1: SEPALS and PETALS FREE TO BASE, SPREADING.

CYLINDRICAL RIBBONROOT *Taeniophyllum cylindrocentrum*
Jul, sporadic. **ID: Roots** flattish, green, flexuose, many growing through air; **peduncle** thread-like, wiry, glabrous; **rachis** bracts triangular, concave, crowded; **flowers** opening singly, whitish/yellow, glabrous; **spur** projected backwards; **ovaries** smooth. Roots 2mm across. Peduncle 20–50mm. Rachis 5–10mm long. Flowers 5–20, c.4 x 4mm. **Dist.:** Qld (CYP – Chester R.); c.200m alt.; also PNG. Single collection on tree in gallery forest. **Status:** Highly localised. **See also:** *T. malianum.*

CAPE YORK RIBBONROOT *Taeniophyllum epacridicola*
Jul–Jan. **ID: Roots** flat, grey/green; **peduncle** thread-like, glabrous; **rachis** zigzagged, rough, bracts triangular, reddish/green; **flowers** pale creamy/yellow with white labellum, opening singly, each lasting 1 day; **spur** in line with labellum; **ovaries** smooth. Roots 4mm across. Peduncle 4–6mm. Flowers c.4.5 x 5mm. **Dist.:** Qld (CYP–N of Jardine R.); 10–100m alt. Coastal lowlands. Twigs and small branches of tall-growing *Leucopogon* sp. on flat tops of stabilised dunes; occas. trees on margins of rainforest. **Status:** Highly localised; rare.

Taeniophyllum cylindrocentrum painting by Cheryl Hodges based on specimens collected in the McIlwraith Ra., Qld.

Taeniophyllum epacridicola near Bamaga, Qld. B. Gray

165

YELLOW RIBBONROOT *Taeniophyllum lobatum*

Aug–Nov. **ID: Roots flat, numerous, pale green to grey/green; peduncle yellowish, hairy; rachis short, usually 2-flowered; flowers opening singly, yellow, initially bell-shaped then opening widely, ovary and outer base of tepals hairy; spur at angle to labellum.** Roots 5mm across. Peduncle 5–15mm. Flowers c.3 x 3mm. **Dist.:** Qld (McIlwraith Ra. to Paluma Ra.); 400–1,250m alt. Ranges and tlnds. Twigs of shrubs and trees in rainforest, often with frequent clouds, mists and fogs. **Status:** Widespread, sporadic.

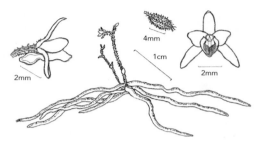

Taeniophyllum lobatum

TANGLED RIBBONROOT *Taeniophyllum malianum*

Sporadic **ID: Tangled clump; roots flat, most aerial, green to grey/green with white spots; peduncle thread-like, glabrous; bracts crowded, 1–3 flowers open at once; flowers yellow, opening widely in evening; spur projected backwards; ovaries smooth.** Roots 3mm across. Peduncle 20–40mm. Flowers 5–15, c.6 x 5mm. **Dist.:** Qld (CYP – Iron Ra., McIlwraith Ra.); 200–600m alt.; also PNG. Streambanks, humid slopes and ridges in sparse scrub and rainforest. Flowers last 1 day, open in spasms, honey-scented. **Status:** Locally common. **See also:** *T. cylindrocentrum.*

WALKER'S RIBBONROOT *Taeniophyllum walkeri*

Apr–Jul. **ID: Roots round, green; racemes short, stubby; peduncle absent or very short, glabrous; rachis slightly zigzagged, bracts large, channelled, glabrous, smooth; flowers opening singly, greenish/yellow, labellum white with reddish markings; spur in line with labellum; ovaries smooth.** Roots 2mm across. Racemes 4–6mm long. Flowers c.4.5 x 4.5mm. **Dist.:** Qld (CYP – W side of McIlwraith Ra.); c.450m alt. Twigs and small branches of native gardenia (*Larsenaikia ochreata*) in open areas near rainforest. **Status:** Highly localised.

Taeniophyllum lobatum, Eungella, Qld. M. Clements

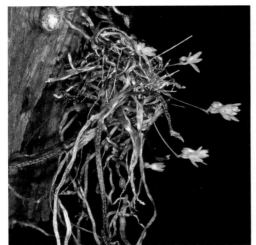

Taeniophyllum malianum, McIlwraith Ra., Qld. B. Lavarack

T. malianum, McIlwraith Ra., Qld. M. Clements

Taeniophyllum walkeri, McIlwraith Ra., Qld. B. Gray

GROUP 2: SEPALS and PETALS FUSED AT SOME POINT ABOVE BASE; FLOWERS WHOLLY TUBULAR OR FORMING FLORAL TUBE AT BASE WITH SPREADING TIPS.

BAUME'S RIBBONROOT *Taeniophyllum baumei*

Apr–Dec. **ID: Plants single or linked clonal colonies; roots round, green; peduncle thread-like, glabrous; rachis zigzagged, bracts in 1 plane; flowers pale green, tubular, tips spreading, opening singly; spur nearly parallel with ovary.** Roots 1mm across. Peduncle 4–8mm. Flowers 5–20, c.3 x 2.2mm. **Dist.:** Qld (CYP–Cape York to McIlwraith Ra.); 10–400m alt. Coast and low ranges. Twigs and small branches of tall-growing *Leucopogon* sp. on flat tops of stabilised dunes; also rainforest trees. Plants spread by root-tip proliferation. **Status:** Highly localised.

CROWDED RIBBONROOT *Taeniophyllum confertum*

Aug–Dec. **ID: Roots flat, dull green; peduncle c. 1mm long, thick; rachis straight, bracts triangular, green, overlapping; flowers tubular, pale green, opening singly, segments not spreading widely; spur in line with labellum; capsules triangular in cross-section.** Roots 2–3mm across. Peduncle c.1mm. Flowers 6–12, c.5 x 2mm. **Dist.:** Qld (McIlwraith Ra., Big Tlnd near Cooktown to Mulgrave R.); 100–700m alt. Lowlands to ranges. Twigs and smaller branches of rainforest trees. **Status:** Localised.

FLAT RIBBONROOT *Taeniophyllum explanatum*

May–Jan. **ID: Roots flat, dull green; peduncle thread-like, glabrous; rachis zigzagged, smooth, bracts at right angles in 1 plane; flowers green, opening singly, segments spreading widely in upper half; spur curved away from labellum.** Roots 1.5–2mm across. Peduncle 12–25mm long. Rachis 3–5mm. Flowers 5–25, c.2.5 x 4mm. **Dist.:** Qld (Mt Windsor Tlnd to Innisfail); 500–1,000m alt. Ranges and tlnds. Shrubs and trees in understorey and upper canopy of rainforest. **Status:** Localised, uncommon.

Taeniophyllum baumei near Bamaga, Qld. B. Gray

Taeniophyllum explanatum, Bridle Ck, Qld. B. Gray

T. confertum, Goldsborough, Qld. B. Gray

CHAIN RIBBONROOT *Taeniophyllum muelleri*

Aug–Oct. **ID: Plants single or linked clonal colonies; roots round, green; peduncle thread-like, glabrous; rachis zigzagged, bracts ovate; flowers tubular, widely spaced, pale yellow/green, opening singly; segments spreading in upper half; spur at an angle to labellum.** Roots 1mm across. Peduncle 30–50mm. Flowers 3–10, c.3 x 2mm. **Dist.:** Qld, NSW (Bamaga to Wauchope); 5–1,200m alt. Lowlands, ranges and tlnds. Shrubs and trees in rainforest and other humid forest, mangroves. Plants spread by root tip proliferation. **Status:** Widespread, common.

TRIANGULAR RIBBONROOT *Taeniophyllum triquetroradix*

Jul–Jan. **ID: Plants single or linked clonal colonies; roots triangular, bluish to grey/green, strongly ridged; peduncle thread-like, glabrous; rachis straight, smooth, floral bracts in 1 plane; flowers green to yellow/green, opening 1 or 2 at a time, segments spreading in upper half; spur in line with labellum.** Roots 1.5–2mm across. Peduncle 5–12mm. Flowers c.4.5 x 3.5mm. **Dist.:** Qld (Mossman to Innisfail); 5–400m alt. Lowlands and ranges. Shrubs and trees in understorey and upper canopy of open rainforest; also mangroves. **Status:** Localised.

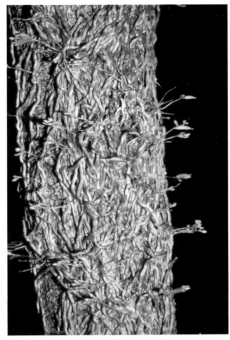

Taeniophyllum muelleri, Craignish, Qld. G. Leiper

T. muelleri, Paluma Ra., Qld. D. Banks

Taeniophyllum triquetroradix, Goldsborough, Qld. D. Titmuss

T. muelleri, Mt Tamborine, Qld. E. Rotherham

Genus *Thrixspermum*

Large diverse genus of c.100 spp. centred in Asia and Pacific, 2 extending to Aust. and *T. carinatifolium* on Christmas Is. (page 218). Sparse to densely clumping epiphytic orchids with numerous roots, erect or pendulous fibrous stems, thick, leathery leaves and racemes arising from stem opposite leaf, apex flattened, bracteate carrying short-lasting flowers (hours). Labellum fixed. NOTES: All plants in locality flower synchronously. Flowers fragrant.

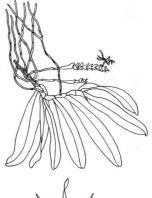

CUPPED HAIRSEED *Thrixspermum congestum*
Sporadic. **ID: Single growth epiphyte; leaves crowded, stiff, yellowish/green; racemes erect, wiry, with crowded spirally arranged bracts; flowers upward-facing, cream/white, 1–4 open at once.** Stem to 150mm. Leaves to 60 x 9mm. Racemes to 100mm. Flowers 12–15mm across. **Dist.:** NT (Melville Is., Bathurst Is.), Qld (Iron Ra. to Tully R.); 0–200m alt.; also PNG, Solomon Is., Indon. Coastal lowlands. Trees in rainforest and mangroves, usually humid airy situations. **Status:** Widespread, common; vulnerable (NT).

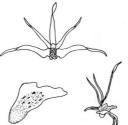

Thrixspermum platystachys

STARRY HAIRSEED *Thrixspermum platystachys*
Sporadic. **ID: Straggly hanging epiphyte; leaves well-spaced, stiff (often yellowish); racemes stiff, apex with 2 ranks of spreading bracts; flowers cream, 1–3 open at once; labellum orange and white.** Stems to 250mm. Leaves to 150 x 40mm. Racemes to 250mm. Flowers 40–60mm across. **Dist.:** Qld (Cape York to Townsville); 0–200m alt.; also PNG, Solomon Is. Coastal lowlands. Shrubs and trees in rainforest and isolated trees near coast. Plants supported by few roots. **Status:** Widespread, locally common.

Thrixspermum congestum, McIlwraith Ra., Qld. D. Banks   *T. congestum*, Goldsborough, Qld. M. Clements

T. platystachys, Russell R., Qld. M. Clements

Thrixspermum platystachys, Daintree, Qld. D. Titmuss

Genus *Trachoma*

About 7 spp., 3 endemic in Aust.; others in Asia, SE Asia, Indon., PNG. Epiphytic orchids with cord-like roots, short stems, thick, leathery leaves and club-shaped racemes carrying short-lasting (hours) flowers in spasmodic bursts. Labellum fixed. NOTES: Fragrant flowers last 1 day and are sometimes produced in large flushes with all plants in an area flowering synchronously. Raceme lengthens between each flowering

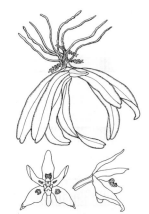

Trachoma stellatum

SHOWY SPECTRAL ORCHID *Trachoma speciosum*

Dec–May. **ID: Upright epiphyte with sparsely branched stems; leaves crowded, pale grey/green to yellow/green; racemes thick, club-shaped; flowers cream, to 15 open at once; labellum orange and white.** Stems to 100mm. Leaves to 140 x 25mm. Racemes to 45mm. Flowers 8–10mm across. **Dist.:** Qld (CYP – Iron Ra., McIlwraith Ra.); 300–600m alt. Ranges. Trees in drier rainforest and rainforest margins, especially trunks and branches of large Hoop Pines. Old plants develop root buttress. **Status:** Highly localised.

STARRY SPECTRAL ORCHID *Trachoma stellatum*

Mar–Jul. **ID: Porrect to pendulous epiphyte with sparsely branched stems; leaves pale green to yellow/green; racemes club-shaped; flowers starry, cream with few purple marks, to 10 open at once; labellum tip yellow.** Stems to 60mm. Leaves to 80 x 20mm. Racemes to 36mm. Flowers 4–5mm across. **Dist.:** Qld (CYP – Iron Ra., McIlwraith Ra.); 400–600m alt. Ranges. Trees on rainforest margins and isolated trees near rainforest. **Status:** Highly localised.

YELLOW SPECTRAL ORCHID *Trachoma subluteum*

Feb–Apr. **ID: Semi-pendulous epiphyte with unbranched stems; leaves dark green, fleshy; racemes thickish; flowers cupped, dull yellow, to 4 open at once; labellum white.** Stems to 60mm. Leaves to 80 x 20mm. Racemes to 15mm. Flowers 3–4mm across. **Dist.:** Qld (Cairns to Innisfail); 50–900m alt. Lowlands to ranges. Rainforest trees, often overhanging streams; ridges with abundant air movement, mists and fogs. **Status:** Locally common.

T. speciosum, McIlwraith Ra., Qld. D. Jones

Trachoma speciosum, McIlwraith Ra., Qld. D. Jones

T. speciosum, McIlwraith Ra., Qld. M. Clements

Trachoma stellatum, McIlwraith Ra., Qld. M. Clements

T. stellatum, McIlwraith Ra., Qld. M. Clements

Trachoma subluteum, Topaz, Qld. D. Jones

T. subluteum, Atherton Tlnd, Qld. D. Titmuss

Genus *Trichoglottis*

Large genus of c.60 spp. centred in Asia and Pacific. One sp. endemic in Aust. Large epiphytic orchids with thick spreading roots, straggly erect or pendulous stems, large leathery leaves and short few-flowered inflorescences that produce flowers in sporadic bursts. Labellum fixed. NOTES: Flowers last a few days.

CHERUB ORCHID *Trichoglottis australiensis*
Nov–May. **ID: Erect to semi-pendulous epiphyte with thick fibrous stems branching from base; leaves numerous, drooping, dark glossy green to yellow/green; racemes short; flowers clustered, creamy/yellow with red blotches.** Stems to 500mm. Leaves to 120 x 25mm. Flowers 2–6, 10–12mm

Trichoglottis australiensis

across. **Dist.:** Qld (CYP – Iron Ra., McIlwraith Ra.); 400–600m alt. Ranges. Trees in dense vegetation along streams; slopes in drier rainforest; boulders in dry but humid gullies. **Status:** Highly localised; vulnerable.

Trichoglottis australiensis, Leo Ck, Qld. M.Harrison

T. australiensis, Lankelly Ck, Qld. D.Jones

Genus *Vanda*

Diverse genus of c.50 spp. centred in Asia and Pacific. One sp. extending to Aust. Large epiphytic orchids with long thick cord-like roots, thick fibrous sparsely branched stems, either flattened strap-like leaves or cylindrical and fleshy and short, few-flowered racemes with moderately large widely opening flowers on long pedicels. Labellum fixed. NOTES: Flowers long lasting.

Vanda hindsi

STRAP ORCHID, CAPE YORK VANDA *Vanda hindsii*

Sep–Mar. **ID: Large epiphyte with thick stems branching from base; leaves numerous, in 2 ranks, strap-like, dark green, thick, leathery; flowers circular, brown, shiny; tepals with yellowish margins; column prominent, white.** Stems to 1m. Leaves to 400 x 40mm. Racemes to 200mm. Flowers 3–7, 30–35mm across. **Dist.:** Qld (CYP – Carron Valley, Iron Range, McIlwraith Ra.); 20–600m alt.; also PNG, Bougainville, Solomon Is. Lowlands to ranges. Exposed trees and rocks in humid forest, often high in tree canopy; among low shrubs on slopes near streams; granite boulders in full sun. **Status:** Highly localised; vulnerable.

Vanda whiteana, FM Hill, Qld. D.Jones

V. whiteana, Kennedy Hill, Qld. D.Jones

MISCELLANEOUS EPIPHYTES

GENERA *ACRIOPSIS, APPENDICULA, BLEPHAROGLOSSUM, BRYOBIUM, CESTICHIS, COELOGYNE, CYMBIDIUM, DIPODIUM, OBERONIA, OCTARRHENA, PHREATIA, PINALIA, THELASIS*

Genus *Acriopsis*

About 12 spp., 1 endemic in Aust.; others in SE Asia through Pacific to PNG. Bulky epiphytic orchids that can be recognised by white aerial litter-trapping roots that form a tangled lattice-like network around small crowded pseudobulbs, each with 2–4 narrow apical leaves. The wiry branching inflorescence, which arises from the base of a pseudobulb, carry small pale flowers that turn yellow before falling.

CHANDELIER ORCHID *Acriopsis emarginata*
Jun–Nov. **ID: Pseudobulbs onion-like, pale green; leaves dark green; panicles arching; flowers small, cream or pinkish; petals spreading widely; lateral sepals fused; labellum white.** Pseudobulbs to 70 x 40mm. Leaves to 200 x 25mm. Panicles to 600mm long. Flowers 4–5mm across. **Dist.:** Qld (Cape York to Daintree R.); 0–300m alt. Rainforest trees, palms, pandans and paperbarks in hot steamy tropical lowland rainforest and swamp forest; occas. extending to intermediate alt. Hosts small biting ants that protect the plant. **Status:** Widespread, common.

Acriopsis emarginata

Acriopsis emarginata, Daintree, Qld. R. Tunstall

A. emarginata, Daintree, Qld. M. Clements

Acriopsis emarginata, Mossman, Qld. M. Harrison

A. emarginata, Daintree, Qld. M. Clements

Genus *Appendicula*

About 60 spp., 1 sp. endemic in Aust.; others in Asia, Polynesia, PNG. Clumping epiphytic orchids with thin leafy fern-like stems (no pseudobulbs), each stem with 2 ranks of alternately arranged leaves and axillary or terminal clusters of small flowers.

STREAM ORCHID *Appendicula australiensis*
Mar–Jun. **ID: Stems upright to pendulous, fern-like, leafy; leaves in alternate pairs, dark green, glossy, thin-textured, base twisted, apex notched; flowers dingy white or greenish/ cream, in clusters of 2–6 along stems.** Stems to 600 x 3mm.

Appendicula australiensis

Leaves to 45 x 15mm. Flowers c.3.5mm across. **Dist.:** Qld (McIlwraith Ra. to Tully R.); 0–700m alt. Rainforest trees overhanging streams; rotting logs, and boulders in humid lowland gullies and riverine vegetation. **Status:** Locally common.

Genus *Blepharoglossum*

About 26 spp., 1 extending to Australia; others in tropical Asia, SE Asia through Pacific to PNG. Epiphytic orchids forming dense clumps of longish thin tapered pseudobulbs each with 1–2 thin-textured leaves and densely flowered apical racemes of small reddish flowers, the thin tepals bent downwards, the labellum sharply decurved near middle. Previously included in *Liparis*. See also: *Cestichis*.

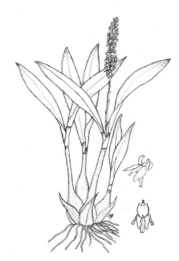

TAPERED SPHINX ORCHID
Blepharoglossum condylobulbon
Dec–Aug. **ID: Pseudobulbs yellow/green, base swollen, tapered to long narrow neck; leaves 2, pale green, thin-textured; racemes stiffly erect; flowers small, pale green/cream with orange/red labellum.** Pseudobulbs to 150 x 20mm. Leaves to 200 x 22mm. Racemes to 150mm. Flowers 15–35, c.4 x 4.5mm. **Dist.:** Qld (CYP –

Blepharoglossum condylobulbon

Iron Ra., McIlwraith Ra.); 300–500m alt.; also SE Asia, Pacific. Rocks and trees on humid slopes and valleys in rainforest. **Status:** Highly localised; vulnerable.

Appendicula australiensis, Mossman Gorge, Qld. D. Banks   *A. australiensis*, Mossman Gorge, Qld. D. Banks

Blepharoglossum condylobulbon, Iron Ra., Qld. D. Titmuss   *B. condylobulbon*, Iron Ra., Qld. R. Tunstall

Genus *Bryobium*

About 150 spp., 4 on mainland Aust., 3 endemic, *B. retusum* on Christmas Is. (page 212); others in tropical Asia and SE Asia extending through Pacific to PNG. Clumping epiphytic orchids with thin much-branched roots, swollen spaced or crowded pseudobulbs, 1–2 fleshy folded leaves and multiflowered racemes from upper nodes carrying small pale glabrous or hairy flowers which often do not open widely. NOTES: Several spp. grow on upper branches of trees high in the rainforest canopy, others on rocks and boulders. Many spp. with short-lasting self-pollinating dull-coloured flowers that don't open widely. Previously included in *Eria*.

Bryobium eriaeoides

BRITTLE URCHIN ORCHID *Bryobium eriaeoides*
Aug–Oct. **ID: Pseudobulbs widely spaced, cylindrical, fleshy, green; leaves 2, stalked, bright green, thin-textured; racemes erect; flowers small, white to purplish/ mauve, usually remaining closed or cupped, rarely widely open.** Pseudobulbs to 100 x 14mm. Leaves to 200 x 30mm. Racemes to 50mm. Flowers 3–12, c.4mm across. **Dist.:** Qld (Iron Ra. to Paluma Ra.); 20–1,000m alt. Rocks and trees in wetter forest, often close to streams. **Status:** Widespread, locally common.

SPOTTED URCHIN ORCHID *Bryobium intermedium*
Oct–Dec. **ID: Pseudobulbs crowded, elliptical in cross section, when young covered by white papery bracts; leaf single, green, thin-textured but leathery; racemes erect, 1 per pseudobulb, often arising beneath leaf; flowers cupped, translucent cream/whitish with few red spots.** Pseudobulbs to 40 x 17mm. Leaf to 135 x 35mm. Racemes to 80mm. Flowers 4–8, to 9mm across. **Dist.:** Qld (Whitfield Ra. near Cairns); 400–600m alt. Rainforest trees. Elusive, rarely seen sp. **Status:** Highly localised; vulnerable.

SMALL URCHIN ORCHID *Bryobium irukandjianum*
Oct–Dec. **ID: Pseudobulbs small, densely crowded, green, fleshy; leaves 2–3, thick, bright green; racemes erect, short, fleshy; flowers small, crowded towards apex of raceme, whitish/pinkish, hairy; bracts brown, prominent.** Pseudobulbs to 12 x 12mm. Leaves to 120 x 10mm. Racemes to 15mm. Flowers 7–12, c.3mm across. **Dist.:** Qld (McIlwraith Ra. to Atherton Tlnd); 500–1,000m alt. Upper branches of rainforest trees; also sheoaks in wetter humid forest. Occas. in extensive patches. **Status:** Highly localised; vulnerable.

Bryobium eriaeoides, Ravenshoe, Qld. D. Jones

B. eriaeoides, Ravenshoe, Qld. D. Jones

Bryobium irukandjianum, Big Tlnd, Qld. M. Harrison

B. irukandjianum, Mt Finnigan, Qld. R. Tunstall

DINGY URCHIN ORCHID *Bryobium queenslandicum*

Aug–Oct. **ID:** Pseudobulbs densely crowded, green, fleshy; leaves 2, upright, dark green, thick; racemes arching; flowers small, opening tardily or cupped, pinkish, hairy. Pseudobulbs to 60 x 12mm. Leaves to 120 x 20mm. Racemes to 40mm. Flowers 3–12, c.3mm across. **Dist.:** Qld (McIlwraith Ra. to Tully R. valley); 500–1,300m alt. Trees and rocks in rainforest with buoyant air movement, frequent clouds, rain and mists. **Status:** Widespread, common.

Genus *Cestichis*

About 20 spp., 7 in Australia, 6 endemic; others in Asia, SE Asia, through Pacific to PNG. Epiphytic orchids forming dense clumps with thin roots and short crowded ovoid pseudobulbs (when young covered with bracts) each with 1–3 thin-textured leaves and racemes of small greenish/yellowish flowers (often sour-smelling), the thin tepals bent downwards, the broader labellum sharply decurved near the middle. NOTES: Trees and rocks in rainforest and moist situations in open forest. Pollination by flies that feed on labellum nectar. Previously included in *Liparis*. See also: *Blepharoglossum*.

Cestichis reflexa

TWISTED SPHINX ORCHID *Cestichis angustilabris*

Mar–Jul. **ID:** Pseudobulbs tapered, green; leaf single; racemes erect/arching; flowers pale yellow/green; tepals partially twisted, recurved against ovary; labellum with 2 low yellow ridges extending to bend. Pseudobulbs to 60 x 20mm. Leaf to 300 x 20mm. Racemes to 250mm. Flowers 15–35, to 8 x 3mm. **Dist.:** Qld (Big Tlnd near Cooktown to Paluma Ra.); 200–1,100m alt. (mainly above 800m). Trees and rocks in rainforest, often on sheltered slopes near streams. **Hab.:** Locally common.

YELLOW SPHINX ORCHID *Cestichis bracteata*

Jul–Sep. **ID:** Pseudobulbs dark green, smooth; leaves 2, dark green; racemes erect/arching, with many prominent bracts; flowers pale green/yellow (ageing yellower); labellum with 2 green fused basal calli and 2 parallel yellow/orange ridges. Pseudobulbs to 50 x 25mm. Leaves to 250 x 15mm. Racemes to 200mm. Flowers 7–12, to 13 x 10mm. **Dist.:** Qld (Mt Finnigan to Tully Falls); 1,000–1,600m alt. Trees and rocks on ridges, slopes and gullies in rainforest. **Status:** Widespread, common.

Bryobium queenslandicum, Johnstone R., Qld. J. Roberts

B. queenslandicum, Kuranda, Qld. R. Tunstall

Cestichis angustilabris, Mt Lewis, Qld. D. Banks

C. angustilabris, Mt Windsor Tlnd, Qld. D. Banks

Cestichis bracteata, Mt Lewis, Qld. D. Banks

C. bracteata, Mt Lewis, Qld. D. Banks

FAIRY SPHINX ORCHID *Cestichis coelogynoides*
Nov–Apr. **ID: Pseudobulbs green, deeply grooved,
covered by papery bracts; leaves 2, yellow/green,
thin-textured (also 2–3 leaf-like bracts); racemes
pendulous; flowers wispy, yellowish/green to
whitish; tepals spreading; labellum wedge-shaped.**
Pseudobulbs to 12 x 16mm. Leaves to 150 x 15mm.
Racemes to 200mm. Flowers 8–20, to 14 x 12mm.
Dist.: Qld, NSW (Eungella, Bunya Mtns to Hunter
R.); 50–800m alt. Coast to ranges. Mossy trunks and
larger branches in wetter forests; occas. rocks. **Status:**
Widespread, common.

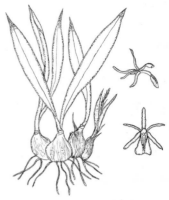

Cestichis coelogynoides

SLENDER SPHINX ORCHID *Cestichis fleckeri*
May–Aug. **ID: Pseudobulbs dark green, fleshy, with wrinkled ridges; leaves 2, dark
green, thin-textured; racemes erect/arching; flowers pale green/whitish (ageing
yellowish); labellum base channelled, with 2 prominent fused orange calli (no ridges).**
Pseudobulbs to 35 x 30mm. Leaves to 350 x 25mm. Racemes to 250mm. Flowers 5–20,
to 12 x 10mm. **Dist.:** Qld (Mt Finnigan to Paluma Ra.); 900–1,600m alt. Trees and rocks
in highland rainforest. **Status:** Locally common.

LARGE SPHINX ORCHID *Cestichis nugentiae*
Sep–Jan. **ID: Pseudobulbs overlapping, green, laterally compressed; leaves 2–4 thin-
textured, dark green to yellow/green; racemes erect/arching; flowers pale yellow/green;
tepals sometimes curled; labellum trowel-shaped with 2 flat orange bands.** Pseudobulbs
to 70 x 40mm. Leaves to 300 x 30mm. Racemes to 250mm. Flowers 8–20, to 17 x
11mm. **Dist.:** Qld (Big Tlnd near Cooktown to Eungella); 600–1,400m alt. Trees and
rocks in rainforest, especially in high altitude zones with frequent clouds and mists.
Status: Widespread, common.

Cestichis coelogynoides,,Washpool NP, NSW. L. Copeland

C. coelogynoides, Washpool NP, NSW. L. Copeland

Cestichis fleckeri, Mt Windsor Tlnd, Qld. M. Harrison

C. fleckeri, Mt Bartle Frere, Qld. D. Banks

Cestichis nugentiae, Mt Baldy, Qld. D. Banks

C. nugentiae, Eungella, Qld. D. Banks

TOM CATS, ONION ORCHID, DOG ORCHID *Cestichis reflexa*

Feb–Jun. **ID: Pseudobulbs green, fleshy; leaves 1–3, dark green to yellow/green; racemes erect; flowers yellow/green; tepals strongly incurved towards ovary; labellum yellow, 2 orange ridges.** Pseudobulbs to 40 x 30mm. Leaves to 300 x 35mm. Racemes to 300mm. Flowers 5–30, to 15 x 10mm. **Dist.:** NSW (Dorrigo to Mumbulla Mtn); 10–900m alt. Coast to ranges. Boulders, cliffs and rock ledges in humid moist/wet forest, rarely on tree trunks. Sharp urine-like floral scent. **Status:** Locally common. **See also:** *C. swenssonii.*

NORTHERN TOM CATS *Cestichis swenssonii*

Feb–Jul. **ID: Pseudobulbs green, fleshy; leaves 1–2, curved, dark green to yellow/green; racemes erect; flowers greenish/yellow; tepals spreading; labellum orange, 2 orange ridges.** Pseudobulbs to 40 x 30mm. Leaves to 200 x 30mm. Racemes to 250mm. Flowers 9–30, to 9 x 10mm. **Dist.:** Qld, NSW (Gympie to Lorne); 100–1,250m alt. Coast to ranges. Shady wet rocks and rock faces in humid forest; edges of escarpments and cliffs. Sharp unpleasant urine-like floral scent. **Status:** Locally common. **See also:** *C. reflexa.*

Genus *Coelogyne*

About 280 species, 1 widespread sp. extending to N Aust. Epiphytic or lithophytic orchids forming large clumps with thin roots, crowded to well-spaced pseudobulbs, 1–2 leaves from apex of pseudobulb and single- to multiflowered racemes arising from emerging new growth or recently mature pseudobulb. Flowers small to large, in 2 ranks along raceme. Australian sp. previously placed in *Pholidota*.

RATTLESNAKE ORCHID *Coelogyne imbricata*

Mar–May. **ID: Pseudobulbs crowded, smooth or furrowed; leaf on petiole c.50mm long, dark green, plicate, thick; racemes wiry, arching/pendulous; flowers with large pinkish concave bracts, in 2 crowded rows, cupped, white, greenish or cream.** Pseudobulbs to 120 x 50mm. Leaves to 400 x 80mm. Racemes to 400mm. Flowers 20–60, c.8 x 7mm. **Dist.:** NT (n), Qld (Moa Is., Dauan Is., Cape York to Townsville); 5–900m alt.; also PNG, Indon., SE Asia, S China. Trees and rocks in wetter forest. **Status:** Widespread, common.

Coelogyne imbricata

Cestichis reflexa, Watagans, NSW. D. Banks

C. reflexa, Dorrigo, NSW. L. Copeland

Cestichis swenssonii, Timbarra Plateau, NSW. L. Copeland

C. swenssonii, Timbarra Plateau, NSW. L. Copeland

Coelogyne imbricata, Tozers Gap, Qld. D. Banks

C. imbricata, Russell R., Qld. M. Clements

Genus *Cymbidium*

About 50 spp., 3 endemic in Aust.; others in Madagascar, Asia, SE Asia, through Pacific to Indon., PNG. Epiphytic or rarely terrestrial orchids forming large clumps with pseudobulbs or slender woody stems, long narrow leaves and multiflowered racemes arising from basal nodes. Flowers right-way-up, small to large, often colourful, with the tepals all of similar shape and size and a hinged or fixed labellum. NOTES: Moist/wet forests, littoral rainforest and trees in swamps. Two native spp. live inside hollow branches containing decaying wood, spreading by rhizomes, the leafy growths emerging as separate clumps from holes in the trunk and larger branches. One of these grows in monsoonal forests and extends inland to sparse forests in low rainfall areas.

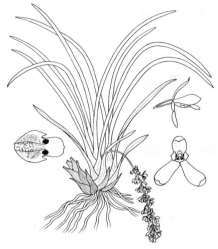

Cymbidium madidum

CHANNEL-LEAF CYMBIDIUM, BLACK ORCHID *Cymbidium canaliculatum*

Sep–Nov. **ID:** Pseudobulbs grey/green; leaves 2–6, rigidly erect/spreading, pale grey/green, deeply channelled; racemes erect/arching/pendulous; flowers variably blotched/striped in different colour combinations; labellum usually white marked with red. Pseudobulbs to 120 x 40mm. Leaves to 500 x 40mm. Racemes to 400mm. Flowers 5–90, to 45 x 40mm. **Dist.:** WA (n), NT (n), Qld (n-s), NSW (s to Hunter R.); 5–900m alt. Drier forests and woodlands on W slopes of dividing range, adjacent semi-arid inland plains, infrequently extending up to 600km inland from coast; occas. near-coastal littoral rainforest, monsoonal thickets and drier coastal forest; trees besides tropical estuaries, coastal bays and escarpments overlooking sea. Commonly on spp. of *Corymbia* and hard-barked *Eucalyptus*. **Status:** Widespread, common.

NATIVE CYMBIDIUM *Cymbidium madidum*

Aug–Dec (–Feb). **ID:** Pseudobulbs large, crowded, green; leaves 4–8, erect/arching, dark green, narrow, strap-shaped, flat; racemes arching/pendulous; flowers green/brownish; labellum white/yellowish marked with red. Pseudobulbs to 250 x 60mm. Leaves to 900 x 40mm. Racemes to 600mm. Flowers 10–70, to 35 x 30mm. **Dist.:** Qld,

Cymbidium canaliculatum, near Collarenebri, NSW. L. Copeland

Cymbidium canaliculatum, Ashford, NSW. D. Banks

C.canaliculatum, Hann R., Qld. D. Banks

NSW (Cape York to Port Macquarie); 5–1,400m alt. Coast to ranges and tlnds. Trees, palms and in clumps of other epiphytes in moist/wet humid forests and swamps; also boulders and cliff faces; rarely terrestrial in near-coastal sand. Sweet floral scent. **Status:** Widespread, common.

SWEET CYMBIDIUM, SNAKE ORCHID *Cymbidium suave*

Aug–Jan. **ID:** Stems crowded, fibre-covered, narrow (no pseudobulbs); leaves 4–8, erect/arching, dark green, narrow, strap-shaped, flat; racemes arching/pendulous; flowers green/brownish; labellum green/yellow, base red.

Stems to 500 x 20mm. Leaves to 450 x 20mm. Racemes to 300mm. Flowers 5–50, to 35 x 20mm. **Dist.:** Qld, NSW (Cooktown to Beowa NP); 1–1,200m alt. Coast to ranges and tlnds, occas. western slopes. Trees, rotting logs and stumps. Common in coastal/ near-coastal moist/wet forest. Sweet/spicy floral scent. **Status:** Widespread, common.

Genus *Dipodium*

About 40 spp., 14 spp. in Aust., mostly leafless terrestrials, 1 sp. is a leaf-bearing climbing epiphyte that produces adventitious roots from its stems; others in Asia, Malaysia, Polynesia, Indon., NG. Small group of terrestrial/epiphytic climbing orchids with fibrous stems (no pseudobulbs), old stems covered with tough dry leaf bases; leaves long, crowded, bases overlapping; racemes multiflowered from upper axils; flowers opening widely, colourful, sepals and petals similar in size and shape; labellum 3-lobed, midlobe hairy.

CLIMBING HYACINTH ORCHID *Dipodium pandanum*

Jul–Dec. **ID:** Stems climbing spirally, with thin, tough adventitious roots, brittle, breaking with age, leafy; leaves crowded, dark green to pale green, dull, thin-textured but tough, strongly ribbed, apex pointed; flowers creamy/white with red external blotches, appearing pink internally. Stems to 5m long. Leaves 200–500 x 30–45mm. Flowers 30–40mm across. Labellum cream/pink with 4–6 red stripes. **Dist.:** Qld (CYP – Iron Ra., McIlwraith Ra.); 200–400m alt; also PNG. Rainforest. **Notes:** Stems climb in a spiral on rocks and trees supported by strong wiry roots. Old leafless stem parts break off and fall to the forest floor where they develop a new shoot, grow through litter, and eventually climb up a rock or tree. Occas. forms localised thickets. **Status:** Highly localised.

Dipodium pandanum

Cymbidium madidum, Coffs Harbour, NSW. L. Copeland

C. madidum, Coffs Harbour, NSW. L. Copeland

Cymbidium suave, Merimbula, NSW. D. Jones

C. suave, Bilpin, NSW. J. Roberts

Dipodium pandanum, McIlwraith Ra., Qld. D. Jones

D. Jones

D. Titmuss

Genus *Oberonia*

About 300 spp., 6 in Aust., 3 endemic, *O. titania* on
Norfolk Is. (page 206); *O. complanata* recently found on
LHI;' others in tropics from southern Africa through Asia
to Pacific, PNG. Epiphytic orchids forming small clumps
of fan-like tufts with thin spreading roots and laterally
flattened leaves that overlap at the base, each tuft similar
to a miniature iris growth. Thin erect to arching racemes
carry whorls of tiny basal bracts and numerous (to c.300)
right-way-up tiny flowers arranged spirally or in whorls.
NOTES: Rainforest, wetter forests, mangroves and trees in
swamps. Flowers best observed with hand lens or microscope.

Oberonia palmicola

MOSSMAN FAIRY ORCHID *Oberonia attenuata*
May–Sep. **ID: Pendulous fans of thin-textured dark green sharply pointed leaves;
racemes pendulous with tiny dagger-shaped basal bracts and whorls of 4–6 pale red/
brown flowers; labellum deeply notched.** Leaves 4–7, to 150 x 8mm. Racemes to 150mm.
Flowers c.1.6mm across. **Dist.:** Qld (Mossman Gorge, Whyanbeel); 30–100m alt. Trees in
moist/wet lowland rainforest near streams. Rarely seen. **Status:** Highly localised; critically
endangered.

ROCKPILE FAIRY ORCHID *Oberonia carnosa*
Feb–Jun. **ID: Small upright fans of curved fleshy light green to reddish blunt leaves;
racemes arching/pendulous with tiny basal bracts and whorls of 4–6 orange to orange/
brown flowers; petals toothed.** Leaves 4–6, to 25 x 8mm. Racemes to 60mm. Flowers
c.1.5mm across. **Dist.:** Qld (CYP – Iron Ra., McIlwraith Ra.); 300–700m alt. Trees in
sparse scrub along stream banks and small humid thickets;
trees and boulders in specialised rockpile vegetation. Plants
often exposed to sun. **Status:** Highly localised; vulnerable.

SOUTHERN GREEN FAIRY ORCHID *Oberonia complanata*
Feb–Jul. **ID: Upright fans of yellow/green fleshy leaves;
racemes arching with few small basal bracts and whorls of
4–6 green/cream flowers; labellum notched.** Leaves 4–6,

Oberonia crateriformis, Herberton Ra., Qld. R. Tunstall

Oberonia attenuata, Whyanbeel, Qld. A. Field

Oberonia carnosa, Iron Ra., Qld. M. Harrison

Oberonia carnosa, Iron Ra., Qld. R. Tunstall

O. carnosa, Iron Ra., Qld. M. Clements

Oberonia complanata, Woodburn, NSW. L. Copeland

O. complanata, Woodburn, NSW. L. Copeland

to 150 x 15mm. Racemes to 200mm. Flowers c.2.5mm across. **Dist.:** Qld, NSW (Gympie to Grafton); 5–500m alt, also LHI. Coast to ranges. Trees and rocks in rainforest, coastal scrub, mangroves and humid gorges. Plants in full sun often severely bleached. **Status.:** Widespread, locally common.

RED FAIRY ORCHID *Oberonia crateriformis*
Feb–Jun. **ID:** Upright/arching fans of green/reddish fleshy pointed leaves; racemes arching/pendulous with bristle-like basal bracts and whorls of 8–10 pale red flowers; labellum with crater-like pit. Leaves 4–6, to 80 x 6mm. Racemes to 150mm. Flowers c.1.7mm across. **Dist.:** Qld (Mt Misery near Cooktown to Eungella); 0–700m alt. Trees and rocks in rainforest, riverine forest, sheltered slopes and humid areas in open forest, gorges, coastal scrub and mangroves. **Status:** Widespread, locally common.

NORTHERN GREEN FAIRY ORCHID *Oberonia flavescens*
Feb–Jul. **ID:** Upright fans of green to yellow/green fleshy leaves; racemes arching with few small basal bracts and whorls of 6–8 whitish or yellowish flowers; labellum broadly triangular with fringed margins. Leaves 4–6, to 150 x 20mm. Racemes to 200mm. Flowers c.2.3mm across. **Dist.:** Qld (Iron Ra. to Clarke Ra. near Eungella); 0–900m alt. Trees and boulders in rainforest and mangroves around large streams and estuaries. **Status:** Locally common.

COMMON FAIRY ORCHID *Oberonia palmicola*
Jun–Sep, Jan–Mar. **ID:** Upright/arching fans of grey/green bronze or pinkish pointed fleshy leaves; racemes arching with bristle-like basal bracts and whorls of 4–8 translucent pinkish flowers; labellum red, flat, margins entire. Leaves 5–7, to 80 x 6mm. Racemes to 150mm. Flowers c.1.4mm across. **Dist.:** Qld, NSW (Gympie to Kendall); 10–600m alt. Trees, palms and rocks in rainforest, riverine forest, sheltered slopes, gorges, coastal scrub and mangroves. **Status:** Locally common.

PIT FAIRY ORCHID *Oberonia rimachila*
Feb–Jun. **ID:** Upright/arching fans of green/reddish fleshy pointed leaves; racemes arching/pendulous with bristle-like basal bracts and whorls of 8–10 translucent to pinkish flowers; labellum red with slit-like pit. Leaves 5–7, to 70 x 8mm. Racemes to 140mm. Flowers c.1.6mm across. **Dist.:** Qld (Tozer Ra. to Palmerston); 50–600m alt. Trees and rocks in rainforest, riverine forest, humid areas in open forest, coastal scrub and mangroves. **Status:** Locally common.

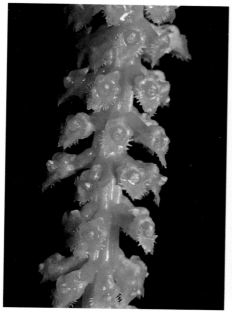

Oberonia flavescens, Daintree, Qld. R. Tunstall

Oberonia palmicola, Middle Brother Mtn, NSW. D. Banks

Oberonia rimachila, Palmerston, Qld. R. Tunstall

O. palmicola, Thora, NSW. L. Copeland

Genus *Octarrhena*

About 20 spp., 1 endemic in Aust.; others in SE Asia through Pacific to Indon., PNG. Tiny clumping epiphytic orchids with monopodial growth habit, thin roots, short sparsely branched stems, short thick fleshy leaves arranged in 2 rows and short racemes carrying tiny upside-down flowers. NOTES: Tiny flowers best examined under a hand lens or microscope.

GRUB ORCHID *Octarrhena pusilla*

Sep–Nov. **ID: Clumping or single-growth epiphyte with erect or curved stems, each stem with cylindrical, curved, fleshy, green to yellow/green leaves; racemes erect, thread-like; flowers cream/white, stalked.** Stems 20–40mm long. Leaves 3–6, to 30 x 2.5mm. Racemes 10–30mm long. Flowers 5–20, c.1.5mm across. **Dist.:** Qld (Big Tlnd near Cooktown to Paluma Ra.); 600–1,400m alt. Rocks and mossy trunks/branches of rainforest trees. Often in local colonies. **Status:** Locally common.

Octarrhena pusilla

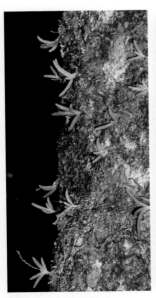

Octarrhena pusilla, Mt Windsor Tlnd, Qld. D. Banks

Octarrhena pusilla, Tinaroo Hills, Qld. J. Fanning

Octarrhena pusilla, Tinaroo Hills, Qld. J. Fanning

Genus *Phreatia*

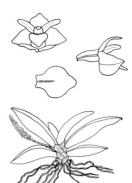

About 180 spp., 2 in Qld, *P. limenophylax and P. paleata* on Norfolk Is. (page 208) and *P. listeri* on Christmas Is. (page 216); others in SE Asia through Pacific to Indon., PNG. Small epiphytic orchids with monopodial growth habit, thin hair-like roots, very short stems (no pseudobulbs), leaves in opposite pairs and racemes of tiny pale flowers. NOTES: Tiny flowers best examined under a hand lens or microscope.

Phreatia micrantha

Phreatia crassiuscula

GREEN CATERPILLAR ORCHID *Phreatia crassiuscula*

Jan–Apr. **ID: Small solitary or clumping epiphyte with short stems; leaves thick, fleshy, dark green, deeply channelled, spreading like a fan; racemes erect to decurved, fleshy; flowers white/cream or greenish, crowded.** Leaves 3–6, to 60 x 10mm. Racemes 15–35mm long. Flowers 20–60, c.2mm across. **Dist.:** Qld (Big Tlnd near Cooktown to Paluma Ra.); 600–1,400m alt. Mossy tree trunks and branches in rainforest and open forest in airy, humid situations. **Status:** Widespread, common.

Phreatia crassiuscula, Mt Baldy, Qld. D. Banks

Phreatia crassiuscula, Mt Baldy, Qld. D. Banks

P. crassiuscula, Tinaroo Hills, Qld. E. Rotherham

FAN ORCHID *Phreatia micrantha*

Oct–Feb. **ID: Single growth epiphyte enlarging each year; base swollen with persistent overlapping leaf bases; leaves in 2 ranks, thin-textured, dark green, spreading like a fan; racemes thin, wiry with tiny cupped white flowers.** Leaves 4–10, to 350 x 25mm. Racemes 200–450mm long. Flowers c.2.5mm across. **Dist.:** Qld (Iron Ra. to Tully R.); 0–400m alt.; also PNG, NCal., Polynesia. Coastal ranges. Rocks and trees in rainforest and humid open forest; mossy branches overhanging streams. **Status:** Locally common.

Genus *Pinalia*

About 20 spp., 2 in Australia, another on Norfolk Is. (page 208); others in SE Asia, Philippines, Indon., PNG. Epiphytic orchids with an intricate network of thin wiry roots, large thick pseudobulbs covered with thin papery sheaths, each with 2–4 leaves and stiffly upright racemes from upper nodes carrying small, hairy flowers. NOTES: Previously included in *Eria*.

Pinalia moluccana

FUZZ ORCHID *Pinalia fitzalanii*

Aug–Oct. **ID: Pseudobulbs crowded, covered with brown sheaths; leaves dark green, thin-textured, stiff; racemes erect to drooping; flowers opening widely, translucent cream to creamy/yellow, hairy.** Pseudobulbs to 200 x 40mm. Leaves 3–4, to 300 x 50mm. Racemes 150–300mm. Flowers 5–35, c.15mm across. **Dist.:** Qld (Moa Is., Dauan Is., Cape York to Townsville); 0–900m alt.; also PNG, Solomon Is. Rocks, trees and palms along stream banks, swamps and humid forests; also mangroves. Flowers fragrant. **Status:** Widespread, common.

GREMLIN ORCHID *Pinalia moluccana*

Aug–Oct. **ID: Pseudobulbs crowded, flattish; leaves dark green, thin-textured, stiff; racemes stiffly upright, hairy; flowers stalked, cupped, hairy, cream/yellowish.** Pseudobulbs to 250 x 30mm. Leaves 3–4, to 350 x 50mm. Racemes 100–300mm. Flowers 15–50, 6–8mm across. **Dist.:** Qld (Iron Ra. to Paluma Ra.); 0–1,000m alt.; also PNG, Solomon Is. Rocks and trees in brightly lit, humid, airy situations close to streams; mangroves on large rivers and estuaries. Previously known as *Eria kingii*. **Status:** Widespread, common.

Phreatia micrantha, Mossman Gorge, Qld. D. Banks

P. micrantha, Iron Ra., Qld. M. Clements

Pinalia fitzalanii, McIlwraith Ra., Qld. D. Jones

P. fitzalanii, Tully, Qld. D. Jones

Pinalia moluccana, Daintree R., Qld. J. Roberts

P. moluccana, Mossman, Qld. D. Banks

Genus *Thelasis*

About 20 spp., 1 in mainland Aust., *T. capitata* on Christmas Is. (page 218); others in Asia, SE Asia through Pacific to Indon., PNG. Clumping epiphytic orchids with thin roots and flattened pseudobulbs; leaves (sometimes appearing absent), either arranged like a fan with overlapping bases or terminal on pseudobulbs; inflorescences arising either in leaf axil or from base of pseudobulb. Flowers small on triangular ovaries.

Thelasis carinata

FLY ORCHID *Thelasis carinata*

Apr–Jun. **ID: Small epiphyte with flattened fleshy stems (no pseudobulbs); leaves erect/arching like a fan, dark green, thin-textured; racemes thin, stiff; flowers tiny, white, on triangular ovaries.**
Stems 20–50mm wide. Leaves 3–6, to 300 x 28mm. Racemes 200–400mm. Flowers 6–15, 3–4mm across. **Dist.:** Qld (CYP – Iron Ra., McIlwraith Ra.); 300–700m alt.; also SE Asia through Pacific to Indon. and PNG. Rocks and trees in rainforest and humid open forest. **Status:** Localised; vulnerable.

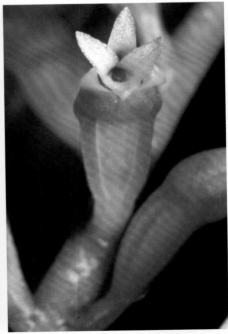

Thelasis carinata, McIlwraith Ra., Qld. M. Clements

T. carinata, Iron Ra., Qld. D. Beardsell

EPIPHYTIC ORCHIDS ON THE MAIN ISLANDS AND ISLAND TERRITORIES

The principal offshore Australian islands and island territories with their own distinctive flora include Lord Howe Island, Norfolk Island, Macquarie Island and Christmas Island. Epiphytic orchid species found on these islands but not occurring naturally on mainland Australia are included here and cross-referenced with generic entries in the main part of the book.

LORD HOWE ISLAND

A tiny subtropical island of some 14.55 square kilometres in the Tasman Sea east of New South Wales. Its flora has many similarities with Norfolk Island and stronger links with New Caledonia and New Zealand than with Australia. Fourteen spp. of orchid occur on Lord Howe Is., including *Thelychiton macropus*, which also occurs on Norfolk Is., *Oberonia complanata*, which also occurs on mainland Aust., and 4 spp. of endemic epiphytes, one an undescribed species related to *Adelopetalum argyropus*. The remaining 9 species of the island's orchids are terrestrials, which are also found in New South Wales.

Genus *Adelopetalum* (see also page 30)

LORD HOWE ISLAND STRAND ORCHID *Adelopetalum* sp. aff. *argyropus*
Mar–May, Aug–Dec. **ID: Pseudobulbs crowded, when young with white felted bracts; flowers nodding, opening widely, cream/yellowish, labellum protruding, orange;**

raceme, ovary and capsule warty. Pseudobulbs to 6 x 5mm. Leaves to 25 x 3.5mm. Racemes 6–15mm. Flowers 1–4, c.4 x 6mm. **Dist.:** Endemic on Lord Howe Is. 100–400m alt. Trees and rocks in wetter forest. **Status:** Highly localised, uncommon.

Adelopetalum sp. aff. argyropus,
Lord Howe Is. G. Walsh

203

GREEN FAIRY ORCHID *Oberonia complanata* from mainland Aust. has recently been found on Lord Howe Is. (see also page 194).

Genus *Plectorrhiza* (see also page 139)

UPRIGHT TANGLE ORCHID *Plectorrhiza erecta*
Oct–Dec. **ID:** Straggly upright plant, roots numerous, coarse, wiry; stem branching from near base; leaves numerous, bright green, fleshy, apex thickened and deflexed; racemes thick, stiffly spreading/arching; flowers red/brown to yellow/orange, cupped, labellum white with few brown marks. Stem to 450mm. Leaves to 45 x 18mm. Racemes to 40mm. Flowers 2–5, 6–8mm across. **Dist.:** Endemic on Lord Howe Is.; 50–450m alt. Shrubby coastal thickets in sand or on rocks. Roots grow through sand, grass and often over the base of fibrous-barked shrubs. **Status:** Locally common.

Genus *Thelychiton* (see also page 106)

YELLOW CANE ORCHID *Thelychiton howeanus*
Jul–Nov. **ID:** Pseudobulbs cylindrical, fattish, furrowed, when young covered with pale sheaths; flowers opening widely, yellow/green ageing pale yellow, with no external red/brown blotches; labellum with pink/red markings. Pseudobulbs to 80cm x 13mm. Leaves 1–6, to 130 x 40mm. Racemes to 150mm. Flowers 5–30, 10–16mm across. **Dist.:** Endemic on Lord Howe Is. Trees and rocks in sheltered humid forest; occas. exposed sites on rocks. **Status:** Locally common. **See also:** *T. gracilicaulis, T. nitidus.*

NORFOLK ISLAND CANE ORCHID *Thelychiton macropus* (see entry for Norfolk Is.). Also occurs on Lord Howe Is.

DROOPING CANE ORCHID *Thelychiton moorei*
Aug–May; **ID:** Pseudobulbs cylindrical, furrowed; flowers tubular with spreading tips, 10–15mm across, crystalline white, tending to droop; labellum slender, without callus ridges. Pseudobulbs to 200 x 8mm. Leaves 2–5, to 150 x 20mm. Racemes to 100mm. Flowers 2–15, 10–15mm across. **Dist.:** Endemic on Lord Howe Is.; 300–875m alt. Trees, rocks and clumps of elkhorn fern in humid sheltered forest; stunted mountain-top moss forest with frequent clouds, fogs and mists. Produces aerial growths. **Status:** Localised, locally common.

Plectorrhiza erecta, Malabar, Lord Howe Is. D. Jones

P. erecta, Lord Howe Is. D. Jones

Thelychiton howeanus, Lord Howe Is. L. Copeland

T. howeanus, Lord Howe Is. L. Copeland

Thelychiton moorei, Lord Howe Is. D. Jones

T. moorei, Lord Howe Is. D. Banks

NORFOLK ISLAND

A tiny subtropical volcanic island of some 34.6 square kilometres in the South Pacific Ocean north-east of Sydney. Its subtropical flora has stronger links with NZ and NCal. than with Australia. Most of the island's orchids are not found on mainland Australia. Twelve spp. of orchid are found on the island, including four sp. of terrestrials that are yet to be confirmed or identified. *Adelopetalum argyropus* and *Thelychiton brachypus* are endemic to the island.

Genus *Adelopetalum* (see also page 30)

SILVER STRAND ORCHID *Adelopetalum argyropus*
Mar–May. **ID: Pseudobulbs crowded, when young covered with white sheaths; flowers not opening widely, sepals and petals very pale yellow; labellum hardly protruding, pale yellow/orange; ovary and capsule sparsely warty.** Pseudobulbs to 10 x 8mm. Leaves to 25 x 6mm. Racemes 10–18mm. Flowers 1–4, c.4 x 3mm. **Dist.:** Endemic on Norfolk Is.; 200–300m alt. Rocks and branches in rainforest. **Notes:** This sp. was originally named using specimens collected in 1804 from Anson Bay on Norfolk Is. Recent morphological studies show that plants recorded from mainland Australia (Qld, NSW) and Lord Howe Is. as *A. argyropus* are actually undescribed. **Status:** Highly localised, uncommon.

Genus *Oberonia* (see also page 194)

SOLDIER'S CREST ORCHID *Oberonia titania*
Jan–Jun. **ID: Upright/arching fans of green, greyish or bronze pointed leaves in iris-like tufts; racemes arching/pendulous with bristle-like basal bracts and whorls of translucent pinkish flowers; labellum red, narrow, cupped, margins entire.** Leaves 5–7, to 60 x 5mm. Racemes to 80mm. Whorls 6–8. Flowers c.1.2mm across. **Dist.:** Norfolk Is.; 10–200m alt.; also NCal. Trees in rainforest and moist humid gullies. **Status:** Highly localised.

Adelopetalum argyropus, Norfolk Is. M. Clements

A. argyropus flowers, Norfolk Is. M. Clements

Oberonia titania, Norfolk Is. M. Clements

Oberonia titania in fruit, Norfolk Is. M. Clements

O. titania, Norfolk Is. M. Clements

Genus *Phreatia* (see also page 199)

NORFOLK ISLAND CATERPILLAR ORCHID *Phreatia limenophylax*
Jan–Apr. **ID:** Small clumping epiphyte with short stems covered by leaf bases (no pseudobulbs); leaves bright green, thick, fleshy, cylindrical, narrowly grooved, spreading like a fan, tip with short asymmetric point; racemes thickish, with curved bracts; flowers resupinate, small, porrect, greenish/white, on plump ovaries. Leaves 4–6, to 60 x 4mm. Racemes 20–30mm long. Flowers c.1mm across. **Dist.:** Norfolk Is. Trees in rainforest. **Status:** Highly localised; endangered.

WHITE LACE ORCHID *Phreatia paleata*
Jan–Apr. **ID:** Clumping epiphyte with crowded globose pseudobulbs; leaves dark green, leathery, flat, blunt, midrib prominent; racemes thickish, arching/drooping; flowers numerous, upside-down, crowded, shortly stalked, white, each subtended by a prominent brownish bract. Pseudobulbs to 20 x 10mm. Leaves 1–2 per pseudobulb, to 250 x 20mm. Racemes to 350mm long. Flowers c.3mm across. **Dist.:** Norfolk Is.; 10–200m alt.; also NCal. Rainforest trees. **Status:** Locally common.

Phreatia paleata

Genus *Pinalia* (see also page 200)

NORFOLK ISLAND FUZZ ORCHID *Pinalia rostriflora*
Aug–Oct. **ID:** Pseudobulbs crowded, covered with brown sheaths; leaves dark green, thin-textured, stiff; racemes erect to arching; flowers opening widely, translucent cream with pale yellow labellum, hairy. Pseudobulbs to 240 x 20mm. Leaves 3–6, to 180 x 30mm. Racemes 50–90mm. Flowers 5–15, c.20mm across. **Dist.:** Qld (Norfolk Is.); c.200m alt.; also PNG, Solomon Is., Pacific Is. Trees in rainforest. **Status:** Highly localised; rare.

Phreatia limenophylax, Norfolk Is. M. Scott

Phreatia limenophylax, Norfolk Is. M. Scott

Phreatia limenophylax, Norfolk Is. M. Scott

Phreatia paleata, New Caledonia. M. Clements

P. rostriflora, Norfolk Is. M. Clements

Genus *Taeniophyllum* (see also page 165)

NORFOLK ISLAND RIBBONROOT *Taeniophyllum norfolkianum*

Aug–Oct. **ID: Roots round, green; peduncle thread-like, glabrous; rachis zigzagged, bracts spreading; flowers tubular, yellow/green, opening singly, segments spreading in upper half; spur more or less parallel with ovary.** Roots 1–2mm across. Racemes 15–25mm. Flowers c.2.2 x 1.5mm. **Dist.:** Norfolk Is.; c.250m alt.; also NZ. Lower trunks and younger leafy branches of large trees of Norfolk Island Pine (*Araucaria heterophylla*). **Status:** Highly localised; vulnerable.

Genus *Thelychiton* (see also page 106)

STUBBY CANE ORCHID *Thelychiton brachypus*

Aug–Oct. **ID: Pseudobulbs stubby, conical, yellow/green; leaves dark green, thin-textured; racemes very short; flowers cream/white to greenish (rarely opening); ovaries thick; labellum peloric, petal-like.** Pseudobulbs to 50 x 8mm. Leaves to 20 x 10mm. Racemes to 7mm. Flowers 2–3, 4–7mm long. **Dist.:** Norfolk Is. (Mt Pitt); 100–300m alt. Trees in humid forest. Flowers remain closed, open partially or open with the tepals remaining cupped. **Status:** Highly localised; endangered. **See also:** *T. macropus.*

Thelychiton brachypus

NORFOLK ISLAND CANE ORCHID *Thelychiton macropus*

Aug–Oct. **ID: Similar to *D. brachypus* but with cylindrical pseudobulbs and longer racemes carrying 5–10 green/yellow or creamy/yellow flowers on thick ovaries; labellum peloric, petal-like.** Pseudobulbs to 350 x 11mm. Leaves to 150 x 25mm. Racemes to 100mm. Flowers 8–10mm across. **Dist.:** Norfolk Is., Lord Howe Is.; 100–300m alt. Trees and rocks in humid forest. Flowers remain closed, open partially or the tepals cupped. **Status:** Locally common; endangered.

Thelychiton macropus

Taeniophyllum norfolkianum Mt Pitt Norfolk Is., M. Clements

T. norfolkianum Norfolk Is., M. Clements

Thelychiton brachypus, Norfolk Is. M. Clements

T. brachypus, Norfolk Is. D. Banks

T. macropus, Norfolk Is. M. Clements

Thelychiton macropus, Norfolk Is. M. Clements

CHRISTMAS ISLAND

A volcanic island of some 135 square kilometres in the Indian Ocean that is administered by Australia. Much of the island is protected as a national park and its flora has strong links with SE Asia. Thirteen spp. of orchid grow naturally on the island including 10 epiphytes, none of which occurs on mainland Australia. Four spp. of orchid are endemic to the island, 2 epiphytic.

Genus *Brachypeza*

About 6 spp., 1 endemic on Christmas Is., others India to PNG. Epiphytic orchids with short sparsely branched fibrous stems, crowded fleshy leaves arranged in 2 ranks and relatively long arching to pendulous racemes with small short-lasting flowers opening in groups. Labellum hinged.

Brachypeza archytas

SAGE ORCHID *Brachypeza archytas*
Oct–Apr. **ID: Clumping sp. with numerous cord-like roots; stems short, upright, often branched from base; leaves yellow/green, arranged like a fan; racemes arching; flowers crowded, white with purple marks.** Leaves to 220 x 25mm. Racemes to 350mm. Flowers 6–8mm across. **Dist.:** Endemic on Christmas Is.; 20–200m alt. Low down on trunks of large trees in tall evergreen rainforest. Flowers last 1–2 days, produced sporadically few at a time in spasms. **Status:** Locally common.

Genus *Bryobium* (see also page 182)

CHRISTMAS ISLAND URCHIN ORCHID *Bryobium retusum*
Sep–Nov. **ID: Plants small; pseudobulbs densely crowded, green, fleshy; leaves 2 erect, bright green, thick; racemes erect, fleshy, hairy; flowers very small, hairy, greenish to whitish with pale brown bracts, in a crowded group at the end of raceme.** Pseudobulbs to 20 x 10mm. Leaves to 130 x 8mm. Racemes to 25mm. Flowers 7–12, c.2mm across. **Dist.:** Christmas Is.; also NG, Solomon Is, Indon., Borneo, NCal. High on trees in rainforest above 200m alt. **Status:** Locally common.

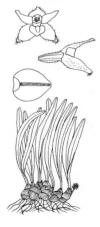

Bryobium retusum

Brachypeza archytas, Christmas Is. D. Jones

B. archytas, Christmas Is. D. Banks

Bryobium retusum, Christmas Is. M. Clements

Genus *Ceraia* (see also page 56)

PIGEON ORCHID, DOVE ORCHID *Ceraia saaronica*
Sporadic. **ID:** Clumping epiphyte with long straggly growths;
pseudobulbs yellowish with narrow upper leafy section (1–3mm
wide); leaves thick, blunt; flowers white; segments thin textured,
margins wavy; labellum white with 5 yellow keels. Pseudobulbs
to 700 x 12mm. Leaves to 80 x 20mm. Flowers c.40 x 40mm.
Dist.: Christmas Is.; also Asia, Pacific. Exposed trees and rocks in
lowland rainforest and beach scrub. Strongly scented, short-lived
flowers (lasting hours) arise sporadically through year and open
simultaneously with other plants in area. **Status:** Widespread,
common.

Ceraia saaronica

Genus *Cleisostoma*

About 90 spp., 1 sp. on Christmas Is., others India to PNG. Epiphytic/lithophytic orchids with
short to long sparsely branched fibrous stems, fleshy/leathery leaves arranged in 2 ranks and
relatively long arching to pendulous racemes with small fleshy flowers opening sequentially.
Labellum hinged.

BEACH ORCHID *Cleisostoma discolor*
Jul–Sep. **ID:** Straggly sp. with thick roots; stems
short, upright, sparsely branched from base; leaves
dark green, apex deeply and unequally bilobed;
racemes pendulous, occas. branched; flowers
uncrowded, pale green to yellowish; tepals with
purple/red central band; labellum white/yellowish
and purple, margins irregularly toothed. Leaves to
230 x 20mm. Racemes to 250mm. Flowers 10–
12mm across. **Dist.:** Christmas Is.; 20–200m alt. also
SE Asia. Trees in beach scrub and rainforest. **Status:**
Uncommon.

Cleisostoma discolor

Ceraia saaronica, Christmas Is. M. Clements
C. saaronica, Singapore City. M. Clements

Genus *Flickingeria* (see also page 98)

CHRISTMAS ISLAND CRIMP ORCHID *Flickingeria nativitatas*

Sporadic. **ID:** Straggly clumps with sparsely branched aerial stems; pseudobulbs smooth, flattened yellow/green; leaves green, leathery; flower single, pale yellow, arising from leaf base; labellum apex irregularly fringed. Stems to 400mm. Pseudobulbs to 40 x 10mm. Leaves to 120 x 20mm. Flowers 10–15mm across. **Dist.:** Christmas Is.; also Java. Rainforest trees on higher terraces of the island. **Status:** Locally common.

Flickingeria nativitatas, Christmas Is. M. Clements

Genus *Phreatia* (see also page 199)

CHRISTMAS ISLAND CATERPILLAR ORCHID *Phreatia listeri*
Sep–Oct. **ID:** Small clumping epiphyte with short stems covered with persistent leaf bases; leaves green to grey/green, narrow, arching/curved, channelled, blunt, spreading like a fan; racemes erect/arching, thin; flowers numerous, very small, shortly stalked, greenish to translucent white. Leaves 4–6, to 110 x 5mm. Racemes 40–80mm long. Flowers c.1.5mm across. **Dist.:** Endemic on Christmas Is. Rainforest trees on higher terraces of the island. **Status:** Locally common.

Genus *Taeniophyllum* (see also page 165)

CHRISTMAS ISLAND RIBBONROOT *Taeniophyllum fornicatum*
Sporadic **ID:** Roots flat or slightly domed, silver/grey to greenish; peduncle hairy to papillate; rachis zigzagged, bracts crowded, overlapping, 1 or 2 flowers open at once; flowers cream/pale yellow, labellum white; spur projected backwards, purple-brown band around opening; anther purple/brown with two white 'eyes'; ovaries smooth. Roots 3mm across. Peduncle 10–20mm. Flowers c.8 x 5mm. **Dist.:** Christmas Is.; 20–200m alt; also Indon. Small branches and twigs of trees in tall rainforest. **Status:** Locally common.

SMALL RIBBONROOT *Taeniophyllum pusillum*
Sporadic **ID:** Roots flat, light-green; peduncle papillate; rachis zigzagged, bracts brown, overlapping, 1 or 2 flowers open at once; flowers bright yellow with white labellum, no colour band around opening to spur and pale yellow anther cap with two brown 'eyes'; spur projected backwards; ovaries smooth. Roots 3mm across. Peduncle 10–30mm. Flowers c.6 x 5mm. **Dist.:** Christmas Is.; 20–200m alt; also Indon., Borneo, Malaysia, Thailand. Trunks and branches of trees in rainforest and mangroves. **Status:** Locally common.

Phreatia listeri, Christmas Is. M. Clements

Phreatia listeri, Christmas Is. M. Clements

Taeniophyllum pusillum, Christmas Is. M. Clements

Taeniophyllum fornicatum, Christmas Is. H. Sweet

Genus *Thelasis* (see also page 202)

CONICAL ORCHID *Thelasis capitata*

Apr–Jun. **ID: Pseudobulbs laterally flattened; leaf single, strap-shaped, dark green, thick, fleshy; racemes from base of pseudobulb, slender, stiff; flowers densely crowded in cone-shaped head, yellowish/green.** Pseudobulbs to 15 x 15mm. Leaf to 150 x 18mm. Racemes 70–180mm. Flowers 5–20, 2.5–3mm across. **Dist.:** Christmas Is.; also Indon. Tall trees in moist/wet rainforest. Flowers open sequentially in a spiral. **Status:** Locally common.

Genus *Thrixspermum* (see also page 172)

CHRISTMAS ISLAND HAIRSEED *Thrixspermum carinatifolium*

Sporadic. **ID: Straggly epiphyte with wiry roots, sparsely branched flattish stems, well-spaced fleshy leaves and stiff wiry racemes with crowded spirally arranged bracts and white flowers (ageing yellowish).** Stems to 300mm. Leaves to 70 x 20mm. Racemes to 240mm. Flowers 17–20mm across. **Dist.:** Christmas Is.; 200–220m alt.; also Malaysia, Indon. Higher branches of tall rainforest trees on upper plateau. Flowers spirally arranged. **Status:** Locally common.

Thelasis capitata, Christmas Is. M. Clements

Thrixspermum carinatifolium, Christmas Is. M. Clements

FURTHER READING

Bishop, T. (2000). *Field Guide to the Orchids of New South Wales and Victoria*, (Second Edition). University of New South Wales Press, Sydney.

Cady, L. and Rotherham, R.R. (1970), *Australian Native Orchids in Colour*. A.H. and A.W. Reed, Sydney.

Copeland, L.M. and Backhouse, G.N. (2022). *Guide to Native Orchids of NSW and ACT*. CSIRO Publishing, Melbourne.

Dockrill, A.W. (1967). *Australasian Sarcanthinae*. Australasian Native Orchid Society, Chipping Norton.

Dockrill, A.W. (1969). *Australian Indigenous Orchids, Vol. 1. The epiphytes, the tropical terrestrial species*. Society for Growing Australian Plants, Sydney.

Dockrill, A.W. (1992). *Australian Indigenous Orchids*, Vols. 1 and 2. Surrey Beaty and Sons, Chipping Norton.

Jones, D.L. (1988). *Native Orchids of Australia*. Reed Books, Australia.

Jones, D.L. (2006). *A Complete Guide to the Native Orchids of Australia including the Island Territories*. Reed New Holland, Sydney.

Jones, D.L. (2021). *A Complete Guide to the Native Orchids of Australia* (Third Edition). Reed New Holland, Sydney.

Jones, D.L., Hopley, T., Duffy, S.M., Richards, K.J., Clements, M.A., and Zhang, X. (2006). *Australian Orchid Genera and Identification System*. CSIRO Publishing, Melbourne.

Jones, D.L., Hopley, T., Duffy. S.M. (2010). *Australian Tropical Rainforest Orchids*. CSIRO Publishing, Melbourne.

Lavarack, P.S. and Gray, B. (1985). *Tropical Orchids of Australia*. Thomas Nelson, Melbourne.

Nicholls, W.H., *Orchids of Australia, Complete Edition* (1969). Edited by D.L. Jones and T.B. Muir. Thomas Nelson, Melbourne.

Upton, W. (1989). *Dendrobium Orchids of Australia*. Houghton Mifflin Australia, Melbourne.

Upton, W. (1992). *Sarcochilus Orchids of Australia*. Double U Orchids, Gosford, NSW.

INDEX TO SCIENTIFIC NAMES

Acriopsis emarginata 178
Adelopetalum argyropum 206
   boonjee 28
   bracteatum 30
   elisae 30
   exiguum 30
   lageniforme 30
   lilianiae 32
   newportii 32
   sp. aff. *argyropum* 203
   sp. aff. *argyropum* 28
   weinthalii
      subsp. *striatum* 32
   weinthalii
      subsp. *weinthalii* 32
Appendicula australiensis 180
Australorchis carrii 60
Australorchis eungellensis 62
   monophylla 62
   schneiderae 62
Blepharochilum
   macphersonii 34
   sladeanum 34
Blepharoglossum
   condylobulbon 180
Bogoria matutina 129
Brachypeza archytas 212
Bryobium eriaeoides 182
   intermedium 182
   irukandjianum 182
   queenslandicum 184
   retusum 212
Bulbophyllum argyropus 206
   baileyi 54
   boonjee 30
   bowkettiae 51
   bracteatum 32
   ciliatum 40
   clavigerum 39
   elisae 32
   evasum 42
   exiguum 32
   gadgarrense 45
   globuliforme 43
   gracillimum 39
   grandimesense 46
   johnsonii 52
   lageniforme 32

   lamingtonense 46
   lewisense 46
   macphersonii 36
   minutissimum 44
   lilianae 34
   nematopodum 50
   newportii 34
   radicans 40
   shepherdii 48
   schillerianum 46
   sladeanum 36
   wadsworthii 48
   weinthalii 34
   whitei 52
   windsorense 48
   wolfei 52
Cadetia clausa 64
   collinsii 64
   maideniana 66
   taylorii 66
   wariana 66
Ceraia macfarlanei 56
   saaronica 214
Cestichis angustilabris 184
   bracteata 184
   coelogynoides 186
   fleckeri 186
   nugentiae 186
   reflexa 188
   swenssonii 188
Chiloschista phyllorhiza 130
Cirrhopetalum clavigerum 37
   gracillimum 37
Cleisostoma discolor 214
Coelandria smillieae 58
Coelogyne imbricata 188
Cymbidium
   canaliculatum 190
   madidum 192
   suave 192
Davejonesia
   aurantiacopurpurea 68
   lichenastra 68
   prenticei 68
Dendrobium adae 106
   aemulum 113
   agrostophyllum 112

   albertisii 85
   aphyllum 59
   aurantiacopurpureum 68
   bairdianum 96
   baileyi 100
   baseyanum 72
   bifalce 104
   callitrophilum 113
   falcorostrum 108
   finniganense 108
   fleckeri 108
   bigibbum 92
   bowmanii 74
   brachypus 210
   brevicaudum 74
   broomfieldii 88
   brownii 86
   cacatua 116
   calamiforme 74
   canaliculatum 90
   cancroides 100
   capitisyork 116
   carrii 60
   carronii 90
   crumenatum 214
   cucumerinum 74
   dicuphum 94
   discolor 86, 88
   dolichophyllum 76
   fellowsii 96
   fairfaxii 76
   fasciculatum 76
   foelschei 92
   gracilicaule 108
   howeanum 204
   insigne 68
   johannis 88
   jonesii 110
   kingianum 110
   lichenastrum 68
   linguiforme 76
   luteocilium 102
   macfarlanei 56
   macropus 210
   macrostachyum 59
   malbrownii 102
   melaleucaphilum 118

   mirbelianum 86
   monophylum 62
   moorei 204
   mortii 78
   nindii 86
   nitidum 110
   nugentii 78
   phalaenopsis 94
   prenticei 68
   pugioniforme 78
   racemosum 80
   rigidum 80
   schneiderae 62
   schoeninum 80
   smillieae 58
   speciosum 112, 114
   striolatum 80
   tattonianum 92
   teretifolium 82
   tetragonum 118
   toressae 105
   tozerensis 102
   trilamellatum 88
   undulatum 86
   wassellii 82
Dichopus insignis 70
Diplocaulobium glabrum 71
Dipodium pandanum 192
Dockrillia banksii 72
   baseyana 72
   bowmanii 74
   brevicauda 74
   calamiformis 74
   cucumerina 74
   dolichophylla 76
   fairfaxii 76
   fasciculata 76
   ×*foederata* 84
   ×*grimesii* 84
   linguiformis var.
      huntiana 78
   linguiformis var.
      linguiformis 76
   mortii 78
   nugentii 78
   pugioniformis 78
   racemosa 80

rigida 80
schoenina 80
striolata subsp.
  chrysantha 82
striolata subsp.
  striolata 80
sulphurea 82
teretifolia 82
wassellii 82
Drymoanthus minutus 131
Durabaculum bigibbum 92
brownii subsp.
  albertisiana ms. 88
brownii subsp.
  broomfieldii 88
brownii subsp.
  brownii ms. 86
canaliculatum 90
carronii 90
dalbertisii 85
dicuphum 94
fellowsii 96
foelschei 92
johannis 88
mirbelianum 86
nindii 86
phalaenopsis 94
×superbiens 96
tattonianum 92
trilamellatum 88
Ephippium ciliatum 38
Eria eriaeoides 182
fitzalanii 200
intermedia 182
irukandjiana 182
moluccana 200
queenslandica 184
retusa 212
rostriflora 208
Flickingeria clementsii 98
convexa 98
nativitatas 214
Fruticicola radicans 38
Grastidium baileyi 100
cancroides 100
luteocilium 102
malbrownii 102
tozerense 102
Kaurorchis evasa 40
Liparis angustilabris 184
bracteata 184

coelogynoides 186
condylobulbon 180
fleckeri 186
nugentiae 186
reflexa 188
swenssonii 188
Luisia atacta 132
corrugata 132
Micropera fasciculata 134
Microtatorchis clementsii 135
Mobilabium hamatum 136
Oberonia attenuata 194
carnosa 194
complanata 194, 204
crateriformis 194
flavescens 196
palmicola 196
rimachila 196
titania 206
Octarrhena pusilla 198
Oncophyllum globuliforme 42
minutissimum 42
Oxysepala gadgarrensis 44
grandimesensis 46
lamingtonensis 46
lewisensis 46
schilleriana subsp.
  maritima 48
schilleriana subsp.
  schilleriana 46
shepherdii 48
wadsworthii 48
windsorensis 48
Papulipetalum
  nematopodum 50
Peristeranthus hillii 137
Phalaenopsis rosenstromii 138
Pholidota imbricata 188
Phreatia crassiuscula 199
limenophylax 208
listeri 216
micrantha 200
paleata 208
Pinalia fitzalanii 200
moluccana 200
rostriflora 208
Plectorrhiza beckleri 139
brevilabris 140
erecta 204
purpurata 140
tridentata 140

Pomatocalpa macphersonii 142
marsupiale 142
Rhinerrhiza divitiflora 144
Robiquetia gracilistipes 145
wassellii 145
Saccolabiopsis armitii 146
rectifolia 146
Sarcanthopsis
  warocqueana 148
Sarcochilus aequalis 150
australis 152
borealis 152
ceciliae 161
dilatatus 154
eriochilus 161
falcatus 149
fitzgeraldii 150
hartmannii 152
hillii 158
hirticalcar 154
loganii 158
niveus 150
olivaceus 154
parviflorus 154
roseus 162
serrulatus 156
setosus 162
spathulatus 156
tricalliatus 158
weinthalii 150
Sayeria bifalcis 104
Schoenorchis micrantha 162
sarcophylla 164
Serpenticaulis bowkettiae 51
johnsonii 52
whitei 52
wolfei 52
Sestochilos baileyi 54
Stilbophyllum toressae 104
Taeniophyllum baumei 168
confertum 168
cylindrocentrum 165
epacridicola 165
explanatum 170
fornicatum 216
lobatum 166
malianum 166
muelleri 170
norfolkianum 210
pusillum 216

triquetroradix 170
walkeri 166
Thelasis capitata 218
carinata 202
Thelychiton adae 106
brachypus 210
cacatua 116
capitisyork 116
carnarvonensis 106
×delicatus 120
falcorostrus 108
finniganensis 108
fleckeri 108
gracilicaulis 108
×gracillimus 120
howeanus 204
jonesii subsp. jonesii 110
jonesii
  subsp. magnificus 110
kingianus 110
macropus 204
macropus 210
melaleucaphilus 118
moorei 204
nitidus 110
×ruppiosus 120
speciosus
  subsp. curvicaulis 114
speciosus
  subsp. speciosus 112
×suffusus 120
tetragonus 118
Thrixspermum
  carinatifolium 218
congestum 172
platystachys 172
Trachoma speciosum 174
stellatum 174
subluteum 174
Trachyrhizum
  agrostophyllum 122
Trichoglottis australiensis 176
Tropilis aemula 123
angusta 124
callitrophilis 124
crassa 124
eburnea 126
eungellensis 126
radiata 126
Vanda hindsii 177

INDEX TO COMMON NAMES

Angular Button Orchid 68
Apricot Cane Orchid 108
Atherton Cane Orchid 110
Banded Butterfly Orchid 156
Banded Tree Spider Orchid 118
Baume's Ribbonroot 168
Beach Orchid 214
Beech Orchid 108
Beetle Orchid 137
Blotched Butterfly Orchid 150
Blotched Cane Orchid 108
Blotched Gemini Orchid 100
Blotched Pineapple Orchid 30
Blotched Sarcanth 142
Blotched Tree Spider Orchid 116
Blotched Wax Orchid 32
Blue Antelope Orchid 86
Blue Mountains Pencil Orchid 76
Bottlebrush Orchid 58
Bridal Veil Orchid 82
Bristly Bells 162
Brittle Urchin Orchid 182
Brown Antler Orchid 88
Brown Butterfly Orchid 154
Brown Rock Orchid 72
Brown Teatree Orchid 90
Brushbox Feather Orchid 126
Buttercup Orchid 122
Butterfly Orchid,
    Gunn's Tree Orchid 152
Canary Orchid 88
Cape York Pencil Orchid 82
Cape York Ribbonroot 165
Chain Ribbonroot 170
Chandelier Orchid 178
Channel-Leaf Cymbidium,
    Black Orchid 190
Cherub Orchid 176
Chocolate Teatree Orchid 88
Christmas Island Caterpillar
    Orchid 216
Christmas Island Crimp Orchid 214
Christmas Island Hairseed 218
Christmas Island Ribbonroot 216
Christmas Island Urchin Orchid 212
Climbing Hyacinth Orchid 192
Closed Burr Orchid 64

Coastal Burr Orchid 66
Common Button Orchid 68
Common Fairy Orchid 196
Common Pencil Orchid 80
Common Snake Orchid 52
Common Tangle Orchid,
    Tangle Root 140
Conical Orchid 218
Cooktown Orchid 94
Crab Orchid 100
Cream Rope Orchid 46
Creeping Brittle Orchid 40
Creeping Burr Orchid 66
Creeping Star Orchid 71
Crimp Orchid 98
Crowded Ribbonroot 168
Cucumber Orchid, Gherkin Orchid 74
Cupped Hairseed 172
Cupped Strand Orchid 32
Curly Pinks 96
Cylindrical Button Orchid 68
Cylindrical Ribbonroot 165
Dagger Orchid 78
Damsel Orchid 96
Dark-Stemmed Antler Orchid 86
Dingy Urchin Orchid 184
Dismal Orchid 134
Drooping Cane Orchid 204
Eungella Ironbark Orchid 126
Eungella Moon Orchid 62
Fairy Bells 161
Fairy Sphinx Orchid 186
Fan Orchid 200
Flared Tree Spider Orchid 118
Flat Ribbonroot 170
Fleshy Flea Orchid 164
Fleshy Snake Orchid 52
Flushed Cane Orchid 120
Fly Orchid 202
Freckle Orchid 129
Fringed Tree Orchid 59
Fruit-Fly Orchid 54
Furrowed Moon Orchid 60
Fuzz Orchid 200
Golden Orchid 86
Golden Rock Orchid 82
Goliath Orchid 148

Gorge Rock Orchid 106
Green Antelope Orchid 85
Green Bead Orchid 42
Green Caterpillar Orchid 199
Green Cowl Orchid 50
Green Midget Orchid 131
Green Pouched Orchid 145
Gremlin Orchid 200
Grooved Velvet Orchid 132
Grub Orchid 198
Harlequin Orchid 154
Hermit Orchid 102
Hermon's Eyelash Orchid 34
Honey Orchid 102
Hook-Leaf 136
Hybrid Pencil Orchid 84
Hybrid Rock Orchid 120
Imp Orchid 139
Ironbark Orchid 123
Large Boulder Orchid 152
Large Oak Orchid 110
Large Pouched Orchid 145
Large Sphinx Orchid 186
Large White Sarcochilus,
    Snowy Sarcochilus 150
Lily-Of-The-Valley Orchid 62
Lord Howe Island Strand Orchid 203
Mainland Strand Orchid 28
Mangrove Pencil Orchid 84
Mangrove Rope Orchid 48
Maroon Strand Orchid 28
Mauve Butterfly Orchid 92
Mcilwraith Burr Orchid 64
Mossman Fairy Orchid 194
Mt Finnigan Cane Orchid 108
Mt Finnigan Pencil Orchid 74
Mt Lewis Rope Orchid 46
Mt Windsor Ribbonroot 135
Myrtle Bells 158
Narrow Thumbnail Orchid 78
Native Bee Orchid 104
Native Cymbidium 192
Native Moth Orchid 138
Norfolk Island Cane Orchid 204
Norfolk Island Cane Orchid 210
Norfolk Island Caterpillar Orchid 208
Norfolk Island Fuzz Orchid 208

Norfolk Island Ribbonroot 210
Northern Fairy Bells 162
Northern Green Fairy Orchid 196
Northern Lawyer Orchid 152
Northern Pencil Orchid 76
Northern Thumbnail Orchid 78
Northern Tom Cats 188
Oak Orchid 110
Orange Blossom Orchid 149
Pale Fairy Bells 158
Pale Rope Orchid 46
Pale Umbrella Orchid 37
Pigeon Orchid, Dove Orchid 214
Piggyback Orchid 98
Pineapple Orchid 30
Pink Rock Orchid 110
Pink Teatree Orchid 90
Pit Fairy Orchid 196
Pouched Sarcanth 142
Purple Sprites 140
Rainforest Feather Orchid 126
Rainforest Rock Orchid 114
Raspy Root Orchid 144
Rattlesnake Orchid 188
Ravine Orchid 150
Red Bead Orchid 42
Red Fairy Orchid 194
Red Horntail Orchid 38
Red Rope Orchid 46
Ribbed Pencil Orchid 82
Rockpile Fairy Orchid 194
Sage Orchid 212
Shaggy Orchid 56
Sheoak Feather Orchid 124
Showy Spectral Orchid 174
Silver Strand Orchid 206
Silver Strand Orchid 206
Skinny Feather Orchid 124

Slender Cane Orchid 106
Slender Feather Orchid 124
Slender Pencil Orchid 78
Slender Sphinx Orchid 186
Small Boulder Orchid 150
Small Butterfly Orchid 156
Small Eyelash Orchid 34
Small-Flowered Pencil Orchid 72
Small Lawyer Orchid 154
Small Moon Orchid 62
Small Ribbonroot 216
Small Tangle Orchid 140
Small Urchin Orchid 182
Smooth Burr Orchid 66
Smooth Strand Orchid 30
Smooth Tongue Orchid 80
Smooth Velvet Orchid 132
Soldier's Crest Orchid 206
Southern Fairy Bells 161
Southern Green Fairy Orchid 194
Southern Lawyer Orchid 154
Southern Teatree Orchid 92
Sparkle Orchid, Mica Orchid 104
Spotted Pitcher Orchid 146
Spotted Urchin Orchid 182
Starfish Orchid 130
Starry Hairseed 172
Starry Spectral Orchid 174
Straggly Pencil Orchid 74
Strap Orchid, Cape York Vanda 177
Streaked Rock Orchid 80
Streaked Wax Orchid 32
Stream Orchid 180
Striped Pyjama Orchid 38
Striped Snake Orchid 51
Stubby Cane Orchid 210
Sweet Cymbidium, Snake Orchid 192
Sydney Rock Orchid, Rock Lily 112

Tableland Pencil Orchid 74
Tangled Flea Orchid 162
Tangled Ribbonroot 166
Tangled Rope Orchid 44
Tapered Sphinx Orchid 180
Tartan Orchid 70
Thin Teatree Orchid 92
Thread-Tipped Rope Orchid 48
Thumbnail Orchid, Tick Orchid 76
Tinaroo Cane Orchid 120
Tiny Pitcher Orchid 146
Tiny Strand Orchid 30
Tom Cats, Onion Orchid,
    Dog Orchid 188
Triangular Ribbonroot 170
Twisted Sphinx Orchid 184
Upright Pencil Orchid 80
Upright Tangle Orchid 204
Walker's Ribbonroot 166
Warty Strand Orchid 32
Wheat Leaf Orchid 48
White Butterfly Orchid 94
White Gemini Orchid 102
White Lace Orchid 208
Wispy Umbrella Orchid 37
Wongi Fairy Bells 158
Yellow Cane Orchid 120
Yellow Cane Orchid 204
Yellow Pencil Orchid 76
Yellow Ribbonroot 166
Yellow Rope Orchid 48
Yellow Snake Orchid 52
Yellow Spectral Orchid 174
Yellow Sphinx Orchid 184
Yellow Teatree Orchid 88
Yellow Tree Spider Orchid 116

Published in 2024 by Reed New Holland Publishers
Sydney

Level 1, 178 Fox Valley Road, Wahroonga, NSW 2076, Australia

newhollandpublishers.com

A record of this book is held at the National Library of Australia.

ISBN 978 1 92151 769 3

Managing Director: Fiona Schultz
Publisher and Project Editor: Simon Papps
Designer: Andrew Davies
Production Director: Arlene Gippert

Printed in China

10 9 8 7 6 5 4 3 2 1

OTHER TITLES BY REED NEW HOLLAND INCLUDE:

A Complete Guide to Native Orchids of Australia (Revised Third Edition)
David L. Jones
ISBN 978 1 76079 627 3

Native Plants of Northern Australia (New Edition)
John Brock
ISBN 978 1 87706 924 6

A Photographic Guide to Wildflowers of Outback Australia
Denise Greig
ISBN 978 1 86436 805 5

Australian Native Plants (Seventh Edition)
John W. Wrigley and Murray Fagg
ISBN 978 1 92554 691 0

Field Guide to Australian Wildflowers
Denise Greig
ISBN 978 1 86436 334 0

Reed Concise Guide: Wildflowers of Australia
Ken Stepnell
ISBN 978 1 92151 755 6

Keep up with Reed New Holland
and New Holland Publishers

 ReedNewHolland
 @NewHollandPublishers and @ReedNewHolland